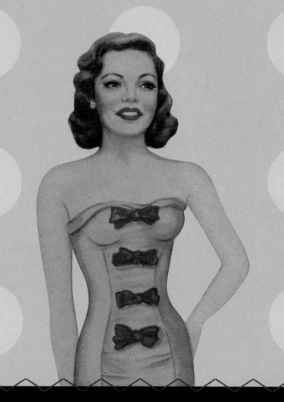

sew what!
SKiRTS

16 SiMPLE STYLES
YOU CAN MAKE
WiTH FABULOUS FABRiCS

FRANCESCA DENHARTOG
& CAROLE ANN CAMP

D&C
David and Charles

A DAVID & CHARLES BOOK

David & Charles is an F+W Publications Inc. company
4700 East Galbraith Road
Cincinnati, OH 45236

First published in the UK in 2007

Originally published in the United States of America by Storey Publishing LLC, 210 Mass
MoCa Way, North Adams, MA 01247, USA.

ISBN-13: 978-0-7153-2695-4 paperback
ISBN-10: 0-7153-2695-3 paperback

Printed in Hong Kong by Elegance
for David & Charles
Brunel House   Newton Abbot   Devon

Visit our website at www.davidandcharles.co.uk

David & Charles books are available from all good bookshops; alternatively you can
contact our Orderline on 0870 9908222 or write to us at FREEPOST EX2 110, D&C
Direct, Newton Abbot, TQ12 4ZZ (no stamp required UK only).

contents

ACKNOWLEDGMENTS

The idea for this book was born out of an excitement for fabric, the need for an easy and approachable skirt formula (no patterns allowed!), and an inspiring phone conversation with Deborah Balmuth at Storey Publishing. Shortly before that fateful phone call, I had put together a three-tiered "bohemian" skirt, using only my waist measurement (a guarded secret) to get me started. I made the skirt in about 45 minutes.

For this book idea, I put together a collection of skirt designs using only a few parameters: no pattern, as little math as possible, and a minimal number of seams. Most have a completion time of less than two hours. Deborah and everyone at Storey Publishing embraced the concept of simple, no-pattern sewing and did wonders with fleshing out all the nuts and bolts.

Special appreciation goes to Carole Ann Camp for providing her technical writing expertise. Without her, this project would have stalled in the early stages. Thanks also to Carol Jessop and Chaila Sekora for jumping in with full enthusiasm and expanding the possibilities with some very creative skirts.

Thanks to Nancy Wood for holding it all together and enhancing every step, while keeping a firm gaze on the vision. Without Sarah Strong, our fearless seamstress who sewed many of the skirts, we would still be wrestling with the first zipper. Many thanks, as well, to all the women who tested the projects at home.

Lastly, I want to thank my women at Valley Fabrics who continue to provide critical advice and sanity when I just can't tell if my ideas have gotten too crazy! And of course, "Thanks, Mom!" for always having a fresh supply of rich, colorful fabrics hanging around the house for me to play with!

introduction

DO YOU FALL IN LOVE WITH A FABRIC, but there isn't enough on the bolt to make curtains? Or maybe your couch is already loaded with pillow experiments? Does your grandmother or mother live too far away to sew for you? Or did she finally rebel against being your sewing slave? Do you refuse to pay over $100 for a simple cotton skirt with an unfinished hem ruffle? "I could make that!" you declare out loud, talking yourself into a territory never before explored.

This book is for the risk-taker who bucks authority and doesn't like being hemmed in by rigid rules, sewing patterns, and instructions. With very little sewing background, some creativity, and some resourcefulness, you can make a playful and wearable skirt tailored to your unique style and shape. This is an opportunity to define your personal style through fabric, color, textures, trims, and buttons, without getting hung up on whether or not your seams are perfect and your stitching is even. Sewing a simple skirt is fun and playful and, most importantly, stress-free!

Using this book as a guide — along with your adventurous spirit — you can sew a variety of skirts to fit any mood, occasion, or event: a casual elastic-waistline tiered skirt, a serious straight skirt, a flirty circle skirt. You are encouraged to blend skirt styles and experiment with finishing touches. This is your chance to make a style statement, minus the sweat and frustration! Once you are familiar with the process, you will be able to finish a skirt project within a couple of hours (unless you have to let the cat out, in, out, et cetera, or get interrupted by the phone). So, go get yourself some funky fabric and rickrack, pick your skirt project of choice, and have some fun!

*I*T IS POSSIBLE TO MAKE all of the skirts in this book with a few basic sewing skills. If you have a new sewing machine but have been afraid to take it out of the box, this book is for you. Even if you have sewn your entire life, you can still find fun and inspiration in these patternless skirts and stylish embellishments.

While none of the skirts are difficult to make, we have arranged them from easiest to easy, with the easiest skirts at the beginning of each chapter. The skirts described in chapters 4 to 7 can be put together — start to finish — in a couple of hours. The skirts in the later chapters, while not more difficult in terms of skill, do take a bit longer to put together. This is mostly because there are more pieces to cut out and more seams to sew.

How to Use This Book

Assumptions

WE ASSUME that you have a basic sewing machine and can find the instruction booklet that came with it! (Replacement manuals can often be found online.) Every sewing machine is different, from your great-grandmother's old treadle machine to today's computerized machines that do almost everything except bring you coffee.

In chapter 2, we describe the basic skills you need to make the skirts in this book. For some specific skills — such as how your particular machine makes buttonholes — refer to your manual. If you have never sewn a stitch on your machine before, or if you've forgotten everything you thought you knew, again, read your manual. Once you can thread your machine and fill the bobbin, get out some scrap fabric and practice some stitching. Try out the zigzag setting, and adjust the machine tension as needed. Take your time, experiment, and have some fun with it!

Your machine probably came with several different presser feet. You will need one for straight stitching and one for zigzag stitching. Sometimes these are two separate feet; sometimes one works for both stitches. If you decide to put in zippers, you will need a zipper foot. You might also have a buttonhole attachment. Get familiar with how all these attachments work.

In Your Sewing Basket

In addition to a sewing machine, you will want to have the following items on hand:

- a good pair of sharp shears used only for cutting fabric
- a pair of pinking shears (which make a zigzag edge) to finish seams and help prevent fraying
- a small pair of scissors for clipping and trimming
- a rotary cutter and mat for cutting long straight lines
- straight pins (glass-head pins are a good choice)
- a tape measure, a wide transparent sewing ruler, and a yardstick
- a variety pack of hand-sewing needles
- a variety pack of sewing-machine needles
- a seam ripper
- seam gauges for pinning hems and making pleats
- disappearing or chalk fabric markers
- a good steam iron and ironing board
- fabric basting glue or basting tape (which washes away)

clipping scissors

rotary cutter

seam gauge

seam ripper

PINS AND NEEDLES

Long straight pins with big heads and very slender shafts are the best for most fabrics. Try not to leave pins in fabric for weeks — you'll be amazed at how fast some nonrust pins will rust! Sewing-machine needles get dull after several hours of sewing. Check your needle regularly for burrs and dull points, and always have spares available. You don't want to have to drive to the store whenever a needle breaks!

SHEAR NONSENSE

Technically, you call them scissors when the length is 6" or less and the finger holes are the same size. Shears are usually 7" to 12", with one larger finger hole (to fit two or more fingers). When buying scissors or shears, look for a pair that fits your hand. You'll want something that feels good to you, is easy to open and close, and isn't too heavy. To keep fabric shears sharp, do not use them to cut paper, cardboard, or aluminum foil.

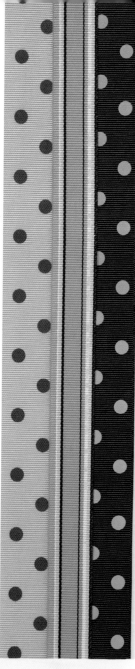

Sewing Jargon

The four most important words you need to know about fabric are *selvage, grainline, bias,* and *nap.*

- The **selvage** (or selvedge) is the finished edge on either side of a woven fabric (not the cut edge). Selvages are designed to keep the fabric from unraveling. Some are white with printed information (see below), some have little holes where the fabric was attached to the loom, some have fringy edges, and some are just plain.

- The **grainline** of the fabric refers to threads running parallel to the selvage. Sometimes this is called the straight (grain) of the fabric. The **crosswise grain** runs from selvage to selvage. You generally want to cut your skirts along the grainline.

- The **bias** runs at a 45-degree angle to the selvage. If you pull fabric along the bias, you will notice that the fabric stretches a lot. If you pull on the straight grain, the fabric does not stretch much.

- When making skirts, **nap** is an important concept to keep in mind. If you run your hand in one direction, the nap is smooth; if you run your hand the opposite way, it feels rough (this is most obvious on velvet). Nap is one way of telling which end of the fabric is "up." On most plain cottons, you will not feel or see nap. However, many fabrics have one-way or *directional* designs, which amounts to the same thing. You will want to cut all skirt pieces with the tops and bottoms going in the same direction.

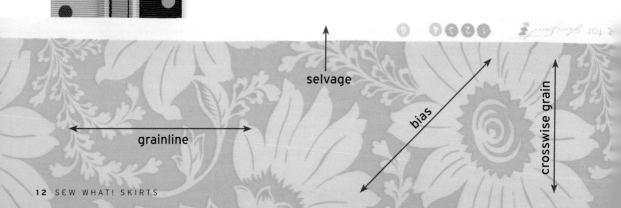

selvage

bias

crosswise grain

grainline

Fab Fabrics, Nifty Notions

Most of the skirts in this book are made from cotton, which is the easiest fabric to sew. If you are new to sewing, you probably want to start with a cotton or cotton blend fabric, leaving the silks, satins, and velvets for later. However, any skirt can be made from just about any fabric. You can start with a plain fabric and decorate it with buttons, trims, or other embellishments such as fancy pockets; or you can select a distinctive fabric to make your fashion statement without a lot of extra add-ons.

pssst...

When buying your fabric, be sure to read the end of the *bolt* (the cardboard that the fabric is wrapped around). There, you will find information about the fabric: what it is made of, how wide it is, and how much it costs per yard. Make a note of the washing instructions for future reference.

Before you make your skirt, prepare the fabric according to the washing instructions. For example, cottons need to be preshrunk before you cut anything out. Wash and dry the fabric in the way you will normally wash it when it becomes a skirt. Although it might be tempting to skip this preparation stage, don't! You will be making the skirt to fit, and you surely don't want it to shrink the first time you wash it.

How Much Fabric to Buy

How much fabric you need to buy depends on you and the skirt you want to make. Although we make recommendations for each skirt, your design choices can change what you need. How long do you want the skirt? How tall are you? How much flare (width at the hemline) do you want?

For most skirts with nap or one-way designs, you will need to purchase two lengths of fabric. A *length* is the approximate distance from your waistline to where you want the hem to be, with a couple of inches added for the hem and seam allowances. For fabrics without nap, you need only a little more than one length, depending on how much flare you want. For example, if you usually wear small to medium sizes and want to make a short straight skirt, you probably need less than a yard of 45" fabric.

NiCE AND SMOOTH

Once you've washed your fabric, it's a good idea to press it before you cut out your skirt. Notice which is the *right* side (outside) of the fabric and which is the *wrong* side (inside).

With right sides together, fold the fabric lengthwise and lay it on a cutting surface. Keep the selvages together and adjust them until there are no bubbles on the folded edge. If the fabric is slippery, you may want to pin the selvages together in a few places to keep it from sliding around.

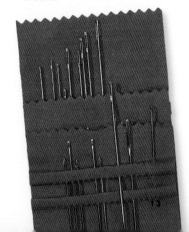

pssst...

NOT-SO-INVISIBLE MARKERS

Not all marking pencils, pens, and chalk will work on all fabrics. Read the manufacturer's directions and test the marker on a scrap of fabric before using it. Make sure the chalk does not bleed through or stain your fabric.

Most cotton fabrics are 42"–45" wide, but some fabrics are as much as 50"–60" wide. We will show you the most likely layout for each skirt in the most common width, but when in doubt, look in a pattern book for a skirt that is similar to the one you want to make, and see how much fabric the pattern recommends for your size.

Threads

Once you've selected fabric for a project, pick up some thread, too. The best all-purpose thread is cotton-wrapped polyester, good for both hand sewing and machine sewing on almost all fabrics. For natural-fiber fabrics, 100% mercerized cotton thread is better. This thread is not good for knits, though, because it doesn't have much stretch. Verify the kind of thread by reading the top of the spool.

Traditionally, thread is closely matched to the color of the fabric, so the stitches won't show. Hold the thread spool next to the fabric to see what works best. If you can't find exactly the right color, go with a slightly darker shade. If you want the stitches to show (for a decorative touch), buy thread in a contrasting color.

Waistline Fasteners

One of the key decisions for any skirt is how to handle the waistline. A gathered waistline is by far the easiest to make and doesn't have to be bulky. The trick is not to have too much fabric bunched up at the waist, which you can address when planning the skirt.

If you don't gather the waistline, you will need to have some kind of opening in one of the seams so you can get the skirt over your hips. Fastener options include the following:

- **Zippers.** Don't be afraid to put in a zipper. It's your best bet for a fitted waistline, and it would be a shame not to try it. We'll show you the easiest way to do it (*see pages 39–40*).

- **Buttons and buttonholes.** Sometimes you'll want a button and buttonhole at the top of a zipper, to secure a waistline. For a wraparound skirt or drawstring opening, you may need a buttonhole on its own. Making buttonholes doesn't have to be hard. Like everything else, it just takes a bit of practice.

- **Hooks and eyes.** When you need a little extra security on a waistband or at the top of a zipper, this is your best choice.

- **Snaps and snap tape.** Snaps can be used instead of hooks and eyes to neaten up a waistline. Snap tape, a marvelous invention, consists of a row of snaps already attached to a strip of fabric tape. Purchased by the yard (or to the length you want), snap tape is easier and quicker to install than individual snaps, and it can be used on some skirts instead of a zipper (*see page* 69).

Embellishments

Now for the real secret to making a unique skirt of your very own design — embellishments! There is no end to what you might try!

- **Bias tapes** are precut, packaged strips of fabric, in a range of colors, that can be used for waistlines, hems, edging, you name it. Because they are cut at an angle of 45 degrees (on the bias), they have some give (or stretch) to them, making them easier to sew around curves.

- **Trims** you can add to your creation are available by the truckload in nearly every fabric store. These include rickracks, laces, ribbons, braids, and beading. Be brave and try something different! Some trims are finished on both edges, and some only on one edge. Finished trims such as rickrack can be topstitched directly onto the fabric. One-edged trims should be sewn with the unfinished edge underneath the fabric edge or into a seam.

- **Buttons** come in two basic styles: with holes (sewn on through the holes) or with shanks (sewn on the back through the metal loops). Some buttons are purely functional, and some purely decorative.

REAL WOMEN HAVE CURVES

Most skirts have a slightly curved edge at the waist and the hemline. This is because you, too, have curves, either a little bit or a lot. When figuring out how much curve to add to the waistline of your skirt, the rule of thumb is to measure up from the waist point by ½" to 1", then measure out to the desired width of the skirt. This gives you a guide for drawing that curve.

After drawing a curve for a waistline or hemline, check the corners to make sure they are at a 90-degree angle (roughly). Just lay a ruler in each corner, and adjust your chalk lines as needed.

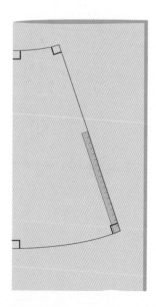

Who Needs a Pattern?

The trouble with commercial patterns is that they are made for a generic person, not for your unique body. You may end up making so many adjustments to a pattern that it's a waste of time and money. Skirts are one of the easiest things to make without a store-bought pattern, so why not jump in and give it a try?

In this book, we show you how to measure and plan your skirt by drawing directly on the fabric or by making your own unique paper pattern that can be used again and again. The only measurements you need are your waist, your hips at the widest point, the length from your waist to your hips, and the length you want the skirt to be.

We usually refer to the top of the skirt as the waistline, but in today's fashion, the top of the skirt can sit anywhere from your actual waistline to your hipline. If you like your skirts to ride below the waist, measure that spot for your waist measurement. Fill in the chart on the next page and refer to it whenever you make a skirt.

Ease into It

How loosely or tightly you like your skirts to fit is also up to you. Generally you want to add *ease* (a little extra room) so the skirt isn't totally skintight. Try adding from 1"–2" to your waist measurement and 2"–4" to your hip measurements.

After you have made your first skirt, and before you put in the zipper or elastic, try the skirt on. If it is bigger than you like, take in the side seams. If it is smaller than you like, change the seam allowance to ¼". Mark changes on your paper pattern, so it will be just the way you like it next time. When you find what works for you and your body type, stick with it.

Do What Works

By the way, you might be able to make a pattern from your favorite skirt, if it doesn't have a lot of gathers, darts, or pleats. The best candidate is a straight skirt that fits you well in the waist and the hips. Trace the skirt onto newsprint or wrapping paper, then add ½" for seam allowances. Use this pattern as a template or for basic measurements for the skirts in this book.

The directions on the next two pages apply to most of the skirts (exceptions are the circle and square skirts and some tiered skirts). When you decide which skirt you want to make, the directions will refer to these pages as needed. The first step in each case is to prepare the fabric, fold it in half lengthwise, and lay it on a cutting surface. Or, to make a pattern, apply the steps to a large piece of paper instead.

Take your time and think things through before you cut the fabric. If you're unsure about the measurements, it's better to cut it larger than you think you need and make adjustments later. Check the pattern layout for the skirt and make sure you have enough fabric. If you are very curvy, read about darts on page 27.

YOUR ViTAL STATiSTiCS

The A–D measurements below will be used to draft the skirts on the next two pages. Waistline seam allowances vary depending on the kind of waistline you want. Add 2" for an elastic waistline; add ½" for a fitted waistline

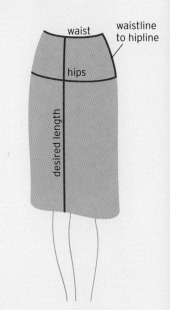

Waist _____ + 2" SA + 1" – 2" ease = _____ ÷ 4* = A _____ inches

Hips _____ + 2" SA + 2"– 4" ease = _____ ÷ 4* = B _____ inches

Waist to hips _____ + _____ SA at waist = C _____ inches

Desired length _____ + 1" hem + _____ SA at waist = D _____ inches

Notes: • **SA** refers to seam allowance, ½" for each seam.

• **Ease** provides a little extra breathing room.

*We divide by 4 because you cut the front and back separately (each is half the skirt) from a folded fabric (which divides it in half again).

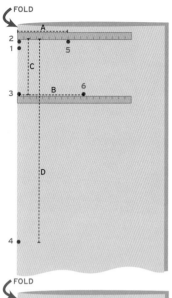

Straight Skirt, Fitted Waist

Draw directly on the fabric or on a large sheet of paper (for instance, the back of wrapping paper) to make a pattern.

Along the fold:

1. Near the top, mark a spot for the waistline.

2. Mark ½"–1" above the first mark (to plot the waistline curve).

3. Mark the distance from waist to hip (measurement C).

4. Mark the desired length (measurement D).

For the side seam:

5. From mark 2, place a ruler perpendicular to the fold and mark the waist width (measurement A).

6. From mark 3, place a ruler perpendicular to the fold and mark the hip width (measurement B).

Connect the dots:

1. **Waist:** Draw a curved line from 1 to 5.

2. **Hemline:** Place a ruler perpendicular to the fold at 4 and draw a line that extends to where the seamline will be. This is an approximation; you can adjust it later.

3. **Side seam:** Draw a straight line from 5 to 6.

4. **Side seam:** Draw a line parallel to the fold and selvage, from 6 to the approximate hemline.

Finishing up:

1. Draw a curved line to smooth out the corner at mark 6.

2. Use your yardstick to check that the distance from the waist to the hemline is consistent.

Cut it out:

For a side zipper: cut two identical pieces (for front and back).
For a back zipper: position the first piece (or pattern) ½" from the fold line or selvages to allow for seam allowance in the back. Cut two back halves.

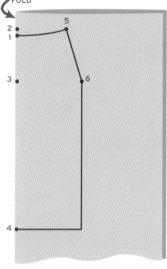

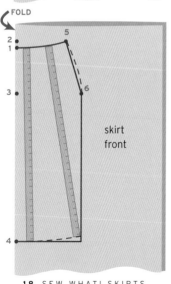

skirt front

THiNK AHEAD

Before you cut, make sure you have enough fabric for both front and back pieces. Depending on the skirt style and your size, you may need only one length of fabric (*see page 13*), or you may need two.

A-Line Skirt, Fitted Waist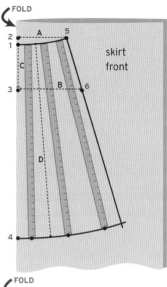

Draw directly on the fabric or on a large sheet of paper to make a pattern. Make the same six marks as for the Straight Skirt, but connect them as follows.

Connect the dots:

1. **Waist:** Draw a curved line from 1 to 5.

2. **Side seam:** Draw a straight line from 5 through 6. Continue to about where the hem will be.

3. **Hemline:** With a yardstick, mark your D measurement from the waistline curve at several points. Connect the points to draw a curve for the hemline.

Cut it out:

For a side zipper: cut two identical pieces (for front and back). **For a back zipper:** position the first piece (or pattern) ½" from the fold line or selvages to allow for seam allowance in the back. Cut two halves for the back.

A-Line Skirt, Elastic Waist ➡

Because you pull the skirt on over your hips, the waistline is based on your hips (B) instead of your waist (A). The D measurement is the desired length plus 1" (hem) and 2" (waist-line casing). Cut two identical pieces (for front and back).

Along the fold:

1. Near the top, mark a spot for the waistline.

2. Mark ½"–1" above the first mark (to plot the waistline curve).

3. Mark the desired length; the D measurement is the desired length plus 1" (for the hem) and 2" (for the elastic waistline).

For the side seam:

4. From mark 2, place a ruler perpendicular to the fold and mark the hip width (measurement B).

Connect the dots: ➡

1. **Waist:** Draw a curved line from 1 to 4.

2. **Side seam:** Draw a straight line from 4, at an angle to the fold, to where it will meet the hemline. The amount of angle depends on your taste and the width of the fabric.

3. **Hemline:** With a yardstick, mark your D measurement from the waistline curve at several points, then connect the points.

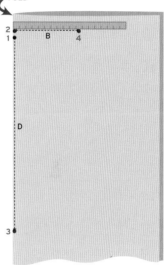

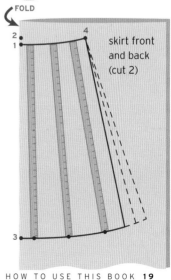

YOU KNOW THE WONDERFUL THING about making a skirt these days? You can be as creative or as simple as you want. Anything goes! At this time in fashion history, you can dream up any combination of colors, embellishments, and fabrics to express your own unique personality.

Believe it or not, you need only a few basic skills to sew the skirts in this book. Some techniques might seem intimidating at first, but only because they are unfamiliar. Once you've tried them a time or two, you'll gain confidence. If you already know the basics, jump on ahead and find a skirt you want to make. Refer back to this chapter as needed if you're not sure about some of the techniques.

Stitch Jargon

WITH SO MANY DIFFERENT SEWING MACHINES out there, we can't tell you how to operate yours. Your sewing-machine manual and an experienced friend or family member can get you started. The rest is just practice.

Most machines have the same basic settings that can be changed by turning a stitch length dial. Be sure to read the section in your manual on stitch length and tension. Here's a quick review of stitches and what they're good for.

- For most straight seams, sew with a **normal stitch** (10–12 stitches per inch). This setting may be highlighted on your stitch length dial.

- A machine **basting stitch** is long, with very few stitches per inch. This stitch is used to hold a seam together temporarily, while you are putting in a zipper or making gathers or ruffles. The stitch is easy to pull out and can be removed later.

- The **zigzag stitch** is used to finish raw edges and for decoration. Your machine manual will show you how to control not only how many zigzag stitches per inch, but also the width of the stitch. You may need a separate zigzag presser foot when using this stitch.

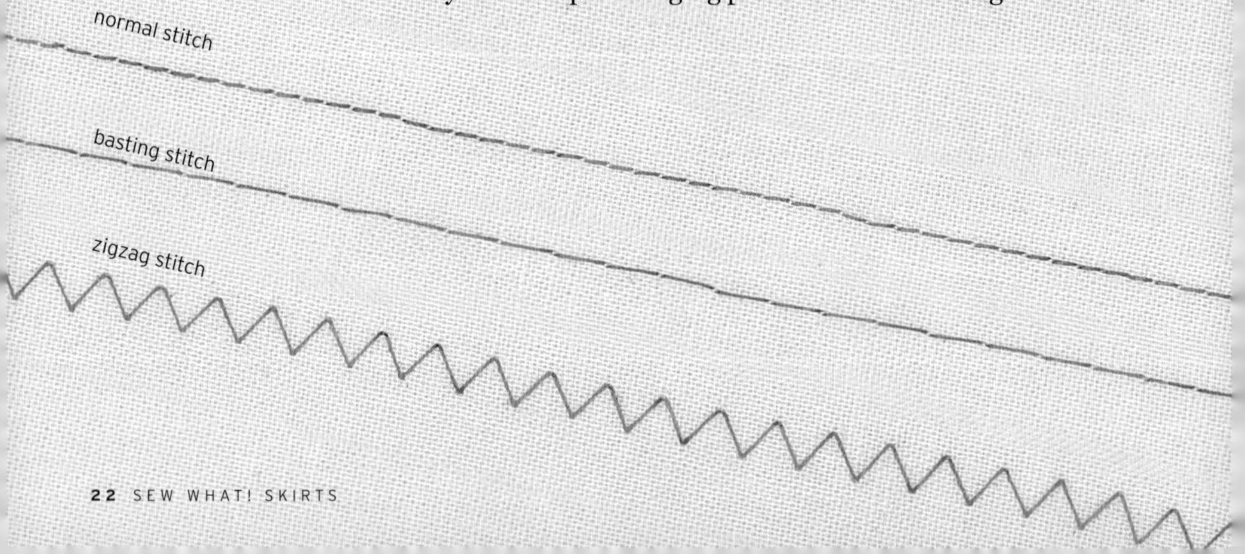

normal stitch

basting stitch

zigzag stitch

The following terms are not stitch settings on a dial; they describe how stitching is used for a particular purpose. In most cases, a normal stitch setting is used.

- A **staystitch** is a line of stitches sewn in the seam allowance almost on the seamline. This stitch can help prevent the seam from coming undone when the seam allowance is clipped.

- **Topstitching** means that the stitching shows on the "top" or the right side of the fabric. This stitch is usually decorative and sewn in one or more straight parallel lines. Topstitching is one option for holding a waistline facing in place. (*See page* 39.)

- **Understitching** does not show and is often used for holding the waistline facing in place. Understitching makes the garment "behave" better, press more easily, and lie flatter. (*See page* 38.)

- **Stitch in the ditch** refers to sewing a line of stitches on top of the stitches in a seam. Ditch stitches are sewn from the right side of the fabric. (*See page* 36.)

- **Backtack stitches** are used mostly at the beginning and end of a line of stitching to prevent the stitching from coming undone. On most machines, you push a button or lever to make the fabric back up, causing stitches to be on top of one another. You don't backtack on basting stitches, as the whole point of basting is to be able to pull out those stitches.

pssst...

HEADS UP!

For the projects in this book, assume a ½" seam allowance, with right sides of the fabric together, unless the directions call for something different.

THE MAGIC NUMBERS

It's a good idea to test your stitch length and tension when starting a new project. You can do this simply by sewing together two scraps of the fabric you'll be using. Check (and adjust as needed) the top thread and the bobbin thread of the stitching to make sure the tension and stitch length are appropriate for that fabric and thread. When the stitches are neither too tight nor too loose, pin a piece of paper to the scrap, labeled with the stitch length, tension, and kind of thread you used. This helps if you are making more than one project at a time or have to leave the project and come back to it later.

Seemly Seams

You probably know that a seam is where you sew two pieces of fabric together. The *seam allowance* is the leftover fabric between the stitching line and the edge of the fabric. Most commercial patterns use a ⅝" seam allowance, and quilters sew with a ¼" seam allowance. We use a ½" seam allowance, mostly because it's easier to do the math! To keep your seam stitching straight, use the guide on the plate of your machine, or put a piece of tape on the plate with the inside edge ½" from the needle.

When sewing a skirt seam, you usually put two pieces of fabric together, with the right sides facing each other. Line up the sides, waist, and hem edges before you sew. Most seams are backtacked at the beginning and end of the seam. Once in a while, you will need to put the wrong sides together or a wrong side of one piece to the right side of another. We'll let you know when!

A standard practice after sewing a seam is to press the seam allowances open. Why? To make the fabric — and therefore your skirt — lie smooth and flat. Sometimes the seam allowances are pressed together. For example, when attaching a waistband, both seam allowances are pressed toward the waistband.

right side

seam

wrong side of fabric

backtack

½" seam allowance

LiNE iT UP!

Most sewing machines have marks to the right of the presser foot to help you measure and align your seams. The longest line is usually at ⅝", the seam width most commonly used. Since we use ½" as our standard, place a strip of tape ½" from your presser foot to keep your seams uniform and straight. (*See left*: We used blue masking tape.) As you move the fabric through the needle, line up the edge of the fabric with the tape.

Finishing Raw Edges

Along the edge of any seam allowance is a raw edge of fabric. This edge will not show, because it's on the inside of the skirt. However, depending on the fabric, this edge could fray or unravel. You'll see for yourself when you prewash the fabric. Some fabric frays very little, and you don't have to finish the edges. Some unraveled edges can be a real mess, bunching up and making your seamlines look bumpy.

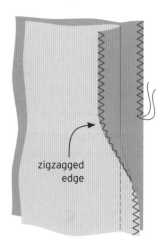

zigzagged
edge

Whether or how you finish those raw edges is entirely up to you. Everyone who sews has a favorite finish. Most purchased garments have serged finishing, which requires a special machine. If you have one, go for it! However, there are plenty of simple alternatives.

- **Zigzag Stitch.** Using the zigzag stitch, sew every raw edge of each seam with the outside point of the stitch at the edge of the fabric.

- **Turned Edge.** This is just what it sounds like — you turn over the edge and stitch it down. For a neat, accurate line, start by sewing a single line of stitching about ¼" from the raw edge. Use this as a guide to fold the edge (toward the body of the skirt); press, then sew another line of stitching close to the fold. As you gain more practice, you will be able to press without a guide — or even skip the pressing altogether and just fold the edge under as you sew.

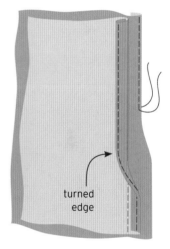

turned
edge

- **Pinking.** Pinking is very easy — it's worth investing in pinking shears. First, sew a straight line of stitching ¼" from the edge. Use pinking shears to cut off the outer edge as shown. This method is particularly good for the bottom of waistline facings because there is no added bulk.

- **Fray Preventer.** There are several fray prevention glues on the market; just follow the directions on the bottle. Be careful with the glue, or you might end up with glue where you don't want it. Place a piece of heavyweight paper between the seam allowance and the fabric to catch any stray drips.

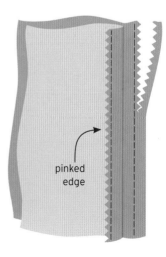

pinked
edge

Sewing a Curved Line

The majority of seams in this book are simple straight seams — a piece of cake. One exception is the circle skirt, which has a wide, attached waistband. In this case, the curved edge of the waistline is sewn to the straight edge of the waistband. Whenever you sew a curved edge to a straight edge, it helps to prepare the edge of the curved piece.

1. Sew a line of staystitching along the curved edge, almost on the seamline but within the seam allowance. In other words, since we're using ½" as a standard seam allowance, stitch a little less than ½" from the raw edge.

2. Every inch or so, carefully clip the seam allowance, up to (but not through) the staystitches. Clipping allows the curved line to stretch a bit, which makes it easier to match it up with a straight line.

3. Now you can pin the curved edge to the straight edge, right sides together. Sew on the seamline, ½" in from the raw edge. If the piece doesn't turn easily or lie flat, clip some more; just be careful not to clip the stitching.

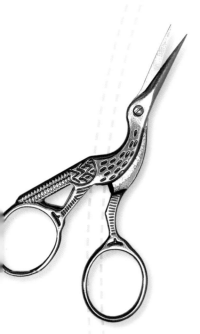

TURN IT UNDER

The width of your hem depends on the project. For most skirts in this book, a ½" double-fold hem is our standard. However, when you make skirts with a great deal of flare, such as a circle skirt, ¼" or less works better. If you were making something like draperies, you might need a 4" to 6" double-fold hem.

Making Darts

For straight skirts and A-line skirts, you might need to make adjustments for tummies and derrieres, especially if you are a curvy gal. If a skirt isn't quite fitting correctly, the solution might be *darts*. Let's say you're making an A-line skirt with a fitted waist. After you put in the zipper and stitch the side seams, try on the skirt. If the waist is too big or the fabric pouches up between your waist and hips, try this.

1. **Placing and pinning the darts.** Turn the skirt inside out and put it back on. In the front of the skirt, pinch in some fabric on either side to get a feel for where the darts need to go. Keep these things in mind:

• Darts are V-shaped, with more fabric at the top and less at the bottom (see illustration). The sides of the V need to be slightly curved lines.

• How many darts you need and their exact location depends on your body. Place them evenly on each side, with the same amount of fabric in each dart.

• For your first pass, put the pins in vertically, to see how the fabric will fit once it's stitched.

• You may need to do the same thing in the back, in which case it helps to have a friend do the pinning.

2. **Sewing the darts**. Take off the skirt. For each dart, place a pin horizontally where the top and the bottom of the dart will be. Then remove the vertical pins; you might want to mark the pin line with chalk before you do so.

On the wrong side of the skirt, sew along the slightly curved line you marked from the top pin to the bottom pin. When you get to the bottom, backtack, then run the stitches right off the edge. Press the darts toward the center of the skirt.

PLANNING AHEAD

If you have the kind of curvy figure that requires darts, you might want to plan for them at the beginning. When calculating your waistline measurement, add another 2 inches or more. The curvier you are, the more you may have to add. The point is to allow enough fabric to work with, so you can make the darts as wide or as often as you need. Plus, if you know where to put your darts, it is easier to stitch them in before you do the side seams.

PLACE THE DARTS

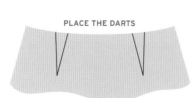

PIN THE DART

SEW THE DART

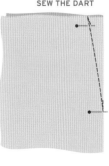

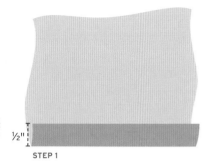

½"

STEP 1

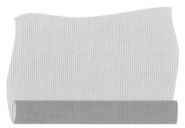

STEP 2

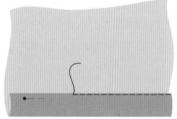

STEP 3

The Bottom Line

The bottom edge of a skirt is called the **hem**. There are several traditional ways to make a hem, and you may invent some ways of your own.

Double-Fold Hem

The hem we use most often in this book is the double-fold hem. This is where a seam gauge comes in handy. Here's how you make one.

1. Fold the bottom edge of the skirt ½" to the inside and press. (For some skirts ¼" may work better.)

2. Fold the hem over another ½" and press again. If you like, put in a few pins to hold the hem in place while you stitch.

3. Stitch as close to the top fold as you can. Some presser feet (check your supplies!) are designed to keep your stitches straight when sewing very close to an edge. With a double-fold hem, the bobbin stitches show on the outside of the skirt, so choose your thread color accordingly.

ZiPPY THREADS

In your grandmother's day, stitches weren't supposed to show. Nowadays, a contrasting thread and a zigzag stitch add style. Fringed hems require a lot of topstitching, so the thread is going to show anyway. You may as well pick a fun color!

Fringed Hem

A fringed hem works well on fabrics with a loose weave — especially if the hemline is cut straight across (without much curve) along the crosswise grain. Here's what you do.

1. Decide how long you would like the fringe to be. For this example, let's say 1".

2. Staystitch and/or zigzag 1" from the edge all around the hem. These stitches will show.

3. To make the fringe, pull the horizontal threads away from the vertical threads. If you pull only one or two threads at a time, they will come out more easily. On a slightly curved edge, you can pull a thread only so far without bunching up the fabric. Just stop and clip the thread before you get into trouble. If you'd rather not fuss, you could just let the unraveling happen as you wash and wear the skirt.

Taped Hem

Another option is to make a hem with iron-on tape. It's easy to use — just press the hem edge under about ½" (or less if there is much curve) and press the tape over it. Unfortunately, it does not work on all fabrics. In spite of the claims, some kinds of tape do come off after several washings, but it's great for emergencies.

For fabrics too bulky for a double-fold hem, or for a neat, finished look, use a ½" seam binding or hem tape. Just stitch one edge of the tape to the hemline of the skirt, turn the hem under about 1", and topstitch or hand-sew the opposite edge of the tape to the skirt.

THE FRINGED HEM ABOVE has a slight curve to it. The fringe is formed by pulling out the horizontal threads (in this case, left to right) until it stops at the stitched line, then clipping off the pulled thread.

*T*HROUGHOUT THE HISTORY OF WOMEN'S FASHION, hemlines are famous for moving up and down with the mood of the times. The same is true for the location of the waistline. At some level, the waistline is an arbitrary concept of the fashion industry, based on the assumption that somewhere around the middle of the female human body there is an indentation.

For centuries, women had themselves strapped into corsets in an effort to achieve the classic hourglass figure. The corset lost popularity in the twentieth century, thank goodness, which left fashion waistlines to roam freely. Today, the top of your skirt can be anywhere you want it to be. Plus, you can opt for a waistband of almost any width or choose not to have a waistband at all.

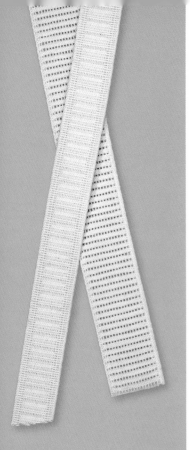

Which Waistline?

There are three basic ways to finish the waistline (top edge) of the skirt. You can make a *waistline casing* for elastic; you can add a *waistband* (literally a strip of fabric sewn on at the waist); or you can make a *facing* (so there is no band at the waist). For most of the skirts in this book, you can substitute one option for another.

Waistline Casing

By far the simplest option is a turned waist, which serves as a *casing* for elastic or a drawstring. Turned edges work best on skirts with very little curvature at the waistline, so they are not a good option for circle skirts. Your bobbin thread will show on the outside of your skirt, so use a color that complements or matches your fabric. Here are the basics for an elastic waistband. See page 48 if you want to try a drawstring.

1. When planning the skirt, allow enough fabric at the waistline to make the casing. (See the illustration below for how to figure this out.) We recommend that you use ½" non-roll elastic. Add ¼" so the casing won't be too tight; that makes ¾". You'll have fabric on both sides of the elastic, so double that number; that makes 1½". Add ½" for the turned-under edge; that equals 2". Therefore, add 2" to the top of the waistline edge before cutting out your skirt.

turned edge ——
back of casing ——
front of casing ——
elastic + ¼"

2. After you've cut out the skirt and sewn the sides together, press the top edge of the skirt under ½".

3. Press the fabric under again, the width of the casing (in our example, that would be ¾"). It helps to also pin the fold after pressing, to keep the fabric from slipping.

4. Sew close to the first folded edge, removing pins as you come to them. When you're back to where you started, stop about an inch short of joining the last stitch to the first. This leaves an opening for inserting the elastic.

5. Cut a strip of elastic the length of your waist, plus 1". Attach a safety pin at one end and thread it through the opening and into the casing. Be careful not to twist the elastic inside the casing.

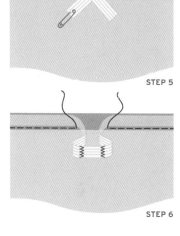

STEP 5

6. Overlap and pin the ends of the elastic together for a minute and try on the skirt. Adjust the tightness of the elastic and repin. Take off the skirt and check again that the elastic didn't get twisted. Pull the elastic out of the casing far enough to zigzag the raw ends using a tight zigzag stitch.

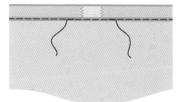

STEP 6

7. Tuck the elastic back into the casing. Topstitch the opening closed by machine, or stitch it up by hand.

STEP 7

ALMOST FEELS LiKE CHEATiNG!

For a stylish, narrow waistband, *bias tape* is a super-easy way to go. No cutting, no folding, no pressing — just sew it on! And there's a bonus. Look carefully at double-fold bias tape and notice that the folded edges do not meet exactly. There is a reason for this. When sewing on bias tape, put the shorter fold of the tape on the outside (right side) of the fabric and the longer fold on the inside (wrong side). When you sew close to the edge from the outside of the skirt, you will automatically be sewing through the bias tape on the back. Some smart woman must have thought of that!

Attached Waistband

A waistband can be cut on the bias from the same fabric as the skirt or from a contrasting fabric; or you can use bias tape. With bias tape, you don't have to worry about sewing a straight edge to a curved edge because the tape has stretch. Bias tape comes in different widths and a variety of colors, so you can find a color that matches or complements your fabric. For best results, we recommend double-fold bias tape.

Bias Tape and Elastic

To use bias tape for an elastic casing, we recommend i"-wide, double-fold bias tape and ¾" non-roll elastic, although ½"-wide double-fold bias tape (with ¼" elastic) will give you more color choices. The elastic should slide through the casing with relative ease and lie flat. The tape is part of the overall look, so choose a color that goes with your skirt fabric.

1. On the inside of your assembled skirt (side seams sewn together), mark with chalk ½" from the waist edge in several places around the waistline.

2. Cut a length of bias tape to match the entire waistline, plus ½" of tape at both ends (to turn under). Beginning at the middle of the back, start pinning the bias tape to the skirt. Sandwich the top of the skirt inside the folds of the bias, with the narrower fold of the tape on the right side of the skirt. (*See the sidebar on page 33.*) Line up the bottom edge of the folded bias tape with the marks you drew in step 1.

STEP 2

3. Where the two ends of bias tape meet in the back, fold the ends under before sewing the tape to the skirt. The ends should just meet, with no overlap. This will become the opening for threading the elastic.

4. From the outside of the fabric and very close to the edge of the tape, carefully stitch the tape to the skirt. Backtack at the starting and ending.

STEP 4

5. Cut a strip of elastic the length of your waist, plus 1". Attach a safety pin at one end and thread it through the opening and into the casing. Be careful not to twist the elastic inside the casing. (*See page* 33.)

6. Overlap and pin the ends of the elastic together for a minute and try on the skirt. Adjust the tightness of the elastic and repin. Take off the skirt and check again that the elastic didn't get twisted. Zigzag the raw ends of the elastic using a tight zigzag stitch. (*See page* 33.)

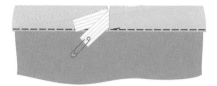

STEP 6

7. Stitch the opening in the bias tape together by hand.

Bias Tape and Zipper

For a skirt with a zipper (in the side or the back) bias tape also works very well. Since you won't be inserting elastic, you can use a narrower width. We recommend ½" double-fold bias tape. You essentially follow the same steps as above, but you place the ends of the bias tape on either side of the zipper. Just tuck in the ends of the tape before you sew. You can hand-sew the ends or, with the right side facing you, stitch very close to the edge of the tape. Add a hook and eye to hold the opening closed. (*See page* 41.)

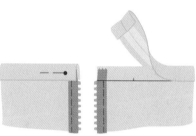

PLACING THE TAPE

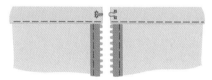

ADDING A HOOK AND EYE

REMINDER!

When you are ready to pin the bias tape to the waist edge, look closely at each folded side of the tape. Which is wider? Be sure to position the wider half on the wrong side (inside) of the skirt.

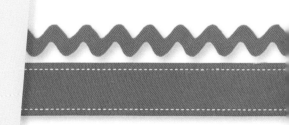

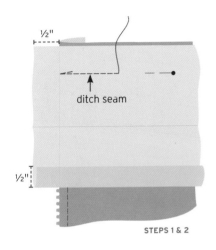

½"

ditch seam

½"

STEPS 1 & 2

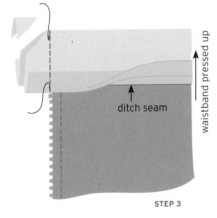

ditch seam

waistband pressed up

STEP 3

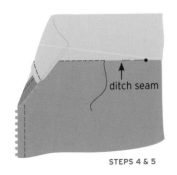

ditch seam

STEPS 4 & 5

Make Your Own Waistband

To make your own waistband, cut a piece of fabric on the straight grain of the fabric, the length of your waist plus 1" (for two seam allowances) and another inch or so for ease. The height of the waistband is whatever you want it to be, times 2 (because you fold it over), plus 1" for seam allowances. (*Note:* For a button and buttonhole, see the next page.)

1. Once you've cut the waistband, fold it almost in half lengthwise, so one side is ¼" wider and the wrong sides are together, and press. Along the wider side, fold the edge under ½" and press.

2. With the right side of the waistband facing the right side of the skirt, pin the unpressed edge of the waistband to the skirt. Leave a ½" seam allowance at each end of the waistband. Sew the waistband in place.

3. Press the waistband and seam allowance up, away from the skirt. Fold the waistband inside out along the pressed fold line, with the right sides together. At each end, stitch the ½" seam allowances together and clip off the top corners.

4. Turn the waistband right side out, with the wrong sides together. The pressed edge (from step 1) should be on the inside of the skirt. Check that the bottom of the folded edge covers the seam attaching the skirt to the waistband. Pin in place from the right side.

5. From the right side, with pins parallel to the seamline, pin in the ditch, catching the underside of the waistband. Make sure the pin heads are to the right, so you will be able to remove them easily as you sew. Stitch in the ditch of the waistband seam, catching the underside of the waistband. (*See page 23*). If this seems too difficult, just hand-sew the back of the waistband to the skirt.

Waistband with a Buttonhole

To make a waistband with a button and buttonhole, the steps are essentially the same as on page 36. The only real difference is the length of the waistband. The back end needs to be long enough to overlap behind the front end. (*See the photo on page* 79.) When you cut the waistband (your waist, plus seam allowances, plus ease), add another 2" for the overlap.

When pinning the waistband to the skirt, just make sure the long end is in the back. For step 3, flatten out the folds when stitching the long end. Line up your horizontal seam with the seam of the skirt, and turn a corner at the end (see illustration at right). Clip the corner and use a ruler or chopstick to turn the end inside out; then proceed to steps 4 and 5 on page 36.

Making a Facing

If you put a zipper in your skirt and don't want a waistband, the solution is to make a facing. This flap of fabric neatly finishes the waistline edge, folds over to the inside, and lies flat. To cut a facing for a skirt, use the skirt pattern piece as a guide. The facing should be about 3" wide and match the shape of the skirt. Cut two pieces, for the front and the back.

Keep in mind that the zipper opening of your skirt should be on the left side (as you wear the skirt). The facing goes on after you have put in the zipper.

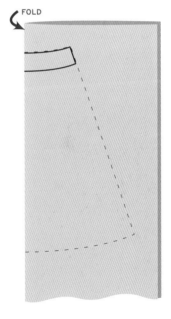

FOLD

1. Put the facing pieces right sides together and sew a seam on only one side of the facing. Finish the seam and press it open. Staystitch the waistline edge of the facing, and do the same with the skirt. Why? You will be clipping the seam allowances later and want to prevent a small clip from becoming a big rip.

2. Stitch ¼" from the bottom edge of the facing, then use pinking shears to trim next to the stitching.

top

½"

staystitch

¼"

STEPS 1 & 2

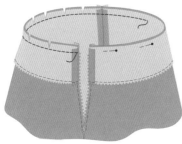

MAKING A FACING, STEPS 3 & 4

3. With right sides together, pin the facing to the skirt waist (the facing will be inside out). Match the opening of the facing with the opening of the skirt. Also match the side seams.

4. Stitch the waistline seam. Every ¾" or so, clip the curves through all layers, right up to the line of stitching. Be careful not to clip the stitching.

To keep your facing from rolling up and showing on the outside, understitch or topstitch the facing to the skirt.

Understitching

With understitching, the stitching doesn't show and the top of the skirt rolls ever so slightly to the inside.

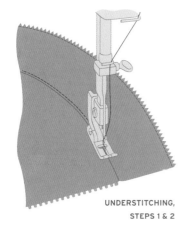

UNDERSTITCHING, STEPS 1 & 2

1. Lay the waistline seam on your ironing board with the facing and both seam allowances to the right and the skirt to the left. Press open, then press the seam allowances toward the facing.

2. Stitch to the right of the seamline but as close to the seam as possible while catching the seam allowances underneath. It may help to use your zipper foot.

3. Fold the facing to the inside and press.

4. On either side of the zipper, fold the ends of the facing to the inside and hand-sew them on both sides.

Topstitching

With topstitching, the stitching will show. This can add an extra line of style to the skirt.

topstitching

1. After clipping the seam allowance, press the facing to the inside.

2. On both sides of the zipper, fold the ends of the facing to the inside and hand-sew them in place.

3. Topstitch as close as you can to the waistline edge of the skirt, through both layers (skirt and facing).

Facing for a Back Zipper

For a skirt with a back zipper, the directions are basically the same. The main difference is that you will have one facing piece in the front and two smaller ones in the back (one on either side of the zipper). To make the two back pieces, cut one piece the same as the front, but make it 1" wider (to allow for extra seam allowances), then cut it in half. For this facing, you stitch, finish, and press both side seams, then turn the back opening under by ½" before stitching the facing to the skirt.

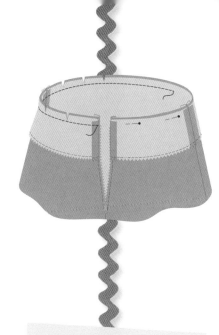

Closing the Gap

As we mentioned in chapter 1, if you prefer a fitted waist over an elastic waistband, you will need some kind of opening to get the skirt over your hips.

Zip It

Putting in a zipper doesn't have to be hard. Really. Like anything else, it just takes practice. While you're learning, it's best to stay away from invisible zippers and stick to the basic steps for a centered zipper, below. The standard zipper length for most skirts is 7"–9".

1. Once you've cut out your skirt pieces and are ready to sew, the first seam to do is the zipper seam. Start by pinning the two pieces together and marking the spot on the left side seam where the bottom of the zipper will be.

2. Start stitching the left-hand seam (with a normal stitch) from the bottom of the skirt to where you marked the bottom of the zipper. Backtack, then finish the seam (where the zipper will be) with a basting stitch. Press the seam open.

INTERFACING MAGIC

If your fabric is really soft or thin, you may want to stiffen up the waistline edge with some iron-on interfacing. This will help it lie flat and not bunch up around the waist. Cut out the interfacing to match the facing pieces, but ¼" smaller on all sides. Press the interfacing to the facings following the manufacturer's directions.

STEP 2

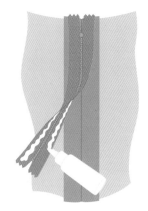

STEP 3

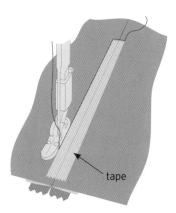

tape

STEPS 4 & 5

FINISHED ZIPPER

3. Apply fabric glue or glue stick (or basting tape) to the right side of the zipper, on either side of the zipper teeth. With the zipper closed, position the top of the zipper head at the waist *seamline, not* at the top of the fabric. Lay the zipper teeth directly over the seamline. Press the zipper down on both sides to affix the glue, then let it dry. If you're nervous about using glue or don't want to use glue on your fabric, you can pin the zipper in place. Remove the pins as you stitch, for a smoother seam.

4. Turn the garment over and lay it flat, right side up. Center a strip of ½"-wide clear tape (the same length as the zipper) over the seam where the zipper is. This will be your stitching guide, so make sure the tape reaches just below the bottom stop of zipper. *Note:* Test the tape first on a scrap of your fabric. If tape is not an option, use chalk and a ruler to make ¼" seamlines on either side of the zipper.

5. Using a zipper foot and starting at the bottom of the zipper at the seam, topstitch across the bottom of the tape. Leave the needle in when turning the corner of the tape, then stitch up the side of the tape. Slide the zipper foot to the other side and repeat on the other side of the tape, also stitching from bottom to top.

6. Pull all threads at the bottom of the zipper to the wrong side and knot them. Remove the basting threads in the fabric in front of the zipper.

Hook It

Whether you've made a waistband or a facing, sometimes you need a little something extra to secure the top of the zipper opening. The simplest solution is a hook and eye. There are little holes on both the hook and the eye/bar so you can hand-sew them to your skirt. (*See page* 35.)

skirt hook & bar

hook & looped eye

skirt hook & bar

- For a facing or narrow bias tape waistband, your best bet is the hook and looped eye. The loop makes it easier to bridge the narrow gap without showing much.

- The skirt hook and bar style is the best choice for wider waistbands because they lay flatter than the other kinds. They are also stronger and can take more wear and tear.

Button It

A custom waistband (not one made from bias tape) can be nicely finished off with a button and buttonhole. You'll need to plan ahead, though, and cut the waistband long enough to overlap at the zipper opening. (*See page* 37.)

Your sewing machine might have a special buttonhole feature (check your manual), but if it doesn't, all you need is a zigzag stitch. There should be directions for that with your machine, too, so we won't go into the details. However, here are a few pointers for a skirt waistband buttonhole:

- Place the buttonhole on the front end of the waistband. Sew the button on the long end on the back. (*See page* 79.)

- The buttonhole should be horizontal, which keeps the button from popping out of the hole as you move around.

- Use a disappearing fabric marker and a ruler to draw where you want the buttonhole to be. Make the horizontal line the exact width of the button you want to use.

- When stitching the buttonhole, leave a narrow gap between the upper and lower horizontal rows of stitching. Then use a sharp seam ripper to slit the gap open. Take care not to cut the long vertical stitches on either end.

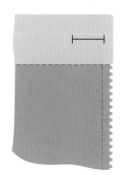

MARKING THE WIDTH

SLITTING OPEN
THE BUTTONHOLE

*I*N 1956, CHRISTIAN DIOR INTRODUCED the A-line skirt. The lines were simple and the shape was more like a trapezoid than an A. However, the name stuck. The original basic A-line skirt had a fitted waist and tummy and derriere darts. The sides continued in a straight line to the hem of the skirt. A-line skirts are generally cut in two to four pieces. Because there are so few pieces to cut, the A-line skirt is one of the easiest skirts to make, requiring only a basic level of sewing skill. We've eliminated the darts, making these skirts even easier to put together.

While one of the simplest skirts to make, they also provide the sewer with opportunities to be creative. As with all skirts, changing the fabric changes the look. Adding trims, buttons, and other embellishments allows the real you to shine through. Go simple or go fancy — your finished skirt is up to you.

We have strayed slightly from Dior's original A-line to include several waistline options. In the skirt we call *Singing the Blues*, there are only two pieces to cut out and no waistband or zipper. In *Meandering Vines*, we've replaced the drawstring with a waistline facing and a side zipper. In *Tourist Trap*, we've moved the zipper from the side seam to a back seam and used vintage material for a completely different look.

The Classic A-Line

Singing the Blues

This simple cotton skirt couldn't be easier to make. The drawstring waist is a cinch, and the drawstring can be made from any number of ready-made cords or ribbons. The lined pocket is trimmed with rickrack, as is the hem. If you don't like rickrack, use a different kind of trim or no trim at all.

Stuff You Need

1¾ yards of 42"–45" fabric

1 spool of matching or contrasting thread

¼ yard of fabric for pocket

1 package of ¾"-wide rickrack

2 yards of cord for drawstring

What You'll Do

Draft the pattern

Cut out the skirt

Pockets with trim

Buttonhole

Straight seams

Waistline casing

Double-fold hem

Add trim

Add the drawstring

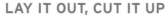

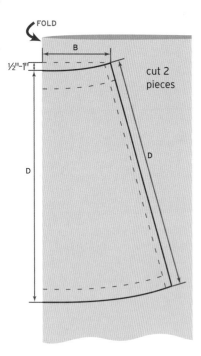

FOLD

B

½"–1"

cut 2
pieces

D

D

D

LAY IT OUT, CUT IT UP

1. Prepare the fabric, then lay it out smooth on a cutting surface. (*See page* 13.) Notice the direction of the nap or pattern design.

2. See chapter 1 for drafting a pattern to fit your size. This skirt pulls on over your hips, so follow the instructions for A-Line Skirt, Elastic Waist. (*See page* 19.) We used a drawstring instead of elastic, but the way you make the skirt is essentially the same. Determine the length of skirt you want, then add 2" for the waistline casing and 1" for the hem.

3. Cut two identical pieces, one each for the front and the back.

PUT IT TOGETHER

1. *Pocket.* It's easier to sew a pocket on before sewing the skirt together, so do it first. Mark and cut out two circles approximately 6"–8" in diameter. A saucer or small plate makes a good template. Also use the edge of the saucer to mark a small section to cut out of the top of the circle.

With right sides together, and using a ¼" seam, stitch the two pocket pieces together. Leave an inch or two open at the bottom of the circle for turning. Clip evenly all around the curves. Clip off the corners where the top meets the sides.

Turn the pocket right side out. Gently push out the seams with the eraser end of a pencil, a chopstick, or a dull table knife. Tuck in the seam allowance at the opening so it doesn't show, and press the pocket flat. Add the rickrack (*see sidebar at right*). When the pocket is done the way you like it, position it on the front of the skirt and sew around the outer curved edge of the fabric (not the edge of the rickrack). Leave the curve at the top completely open for your hand. An extra backtack at the start and finish is a good idea to help the pocket stay put.

2. *Buttonhole.* With a drawstring, you need a buttonhole in front for the ends to come through. To figure out where to put

the buttonhole, you need to think about the casing. As explained in chapter 3 (*see page* 32), you will fold over the waistline edge of the skirt twice. See the illustration to figure out how far down from the top your buttonhole needs to be. Base the casing width on the width of the drawstring you'll be using, plus about ¼".

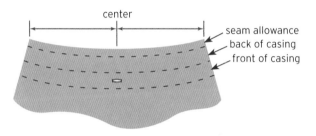

center

seam allowance
back of casing
front of casing

Find the center of the front by folding it in half and marking it with chalk. Now make a horizontal ½"-wide buttonhole. (*See page* 41.)

3. *Side seams.* Put the front and back pieces together, the with right sides facing each other. Sew both side seams in the same direction, top to bottom, using a ½" seam allowance. Finish the seam edges and press the seams open.

WAISTLINE EDGE

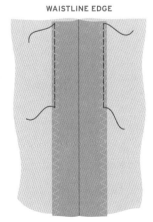

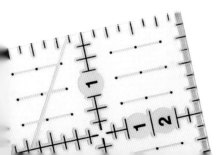

RICKRACKING YOUR BRAIN

When sewing rickrack to the pocket or hem, pin it on the underside of the fabric with the points peeking out. Stitch as close to the edge as possible. Allow some ease on the rickrack while going around curves so the fabric will lie flat and not pop out. For the pocket, it may be easier to put the rickrack on in two sections, with one piece across the top and the other eased around the curve.

THE ADVENTUROUS SEAMSTRESS

If you haven't done much sewing yet, you might want to stick with cotton for starters, because it's easier to work with. However, as you gain confidence, feel free to explore other possibilities. Any time you use something other than cotton, check the end of the bolt for washing and preshrinking instructions.

4. *Waist.* Before you make the casing, tack all seam allowances to the skirt by stitching from the waist edge down about 1½". This will keep the drawstring from getting stuck later when you are threading it through the casing.

Now follow instructions on pages 32–33 for making the casing. Essentially, fold under and press a ½" seam allowance, then fold under and press enough to hold your drawstring. Make sure the buttonhole is centered from top to bottom within the casing.

5. *Hem.* Make a ½" double-fold hem on the bottom of the skirt. (*See page* 28.)

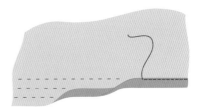

6. *Adding trim.* Pin rickrack to the wrong side of the hem so that the hemline runs through the center of the rickrack. Topstitch the rickrack in place very close to the bottom edge of the skirt.

7. *Drawstring.* The easiest option for a drawstring is to buy a cord of some kind. (Flat cords like the one we use are less bulky and more flattering.) You generally need a drawstring as long as your waist measurement times 2.

Use a safety pin to thread the drawstring through the button-hole opening. Use tape or fray preventer or stitch the ends of the drawstring to keep them from unraveling. Tie a knot to keep them from disappearing back into the casing.

Make Your Own

Here's the easiest way to make a drawstring. Use leftover fabric from your skirt or a complementary lightweight fabric. Err on the side of making it too long — you can always shorten it later. These directions are for a ½"-wide drawstring.

1. A drawstring is pretty long, so you will probably need to cut two lengths of fabric and sew them together. Measure out the length you need (your waist measurement times 2) and cut two strips 2" wide. Put the two strips together, right sides facing. At one end, sew the two pieces together. Press the seams open.

2. With wrong sides together, fold and press the fabric in half lengthwise, then reopen the fabric.

3. Fold both edges in to meet in the center, and press.

4. Refold on the center fold; repress if necessary.

5. Topstitch the full length of the drawstring, as close to the open edge as possible.

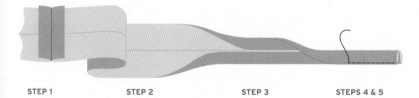

STEP 1   STEP 2   STEP 3   STEPS 4 & 5

6. To finish the ends, simply tie a half knot and let the ends unravel over time. Or, for a neat finish, tuck in the fabric at either end and sew by hand.

taped end

store-bought ———→

custom-made ————————→

Meandering Vines

Sometimes it's just all about the fabric. With an elegant, embroidered cloth like this one, it's hard to go wrong. This style is fitted from waist to hip, made with a side zipper and facing at the waistline. The A-line shape provides fullness from the hips to the hem, and three high-fashion buttons complete the look. Hard to make? No way! Only two main pieces and two facings to cut out.

Stuff You Need

2 yards of 42"–45" fabric

1 spool of matching or contrasting thread

1 matching 7"–9" skirt zipper

Iron-on interfacing (optional)

3 decorative buttons (optional)

Basting glue or tape (optional)

½"-wide clear tape (optional)

What You'll Do

Draft the pattern

Cut out the skirt

Put in the zipper

Straight seams

Waistline facing

Double-fold hem

Sew on buttons

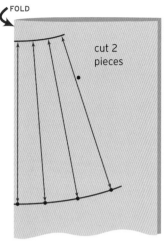

cut 2
pieces

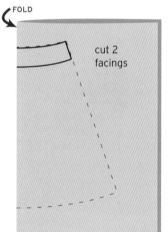

cut 2
facings

LAY IT OUT, CUT IT UP

1. Prepare the fabric, then lay it out smooth on a cutting surface. (*See page* 13.) Notice the direction of the nap or pattern design.

2. Refer to chapter 1 for drafting a pattern to fit your size. Follow the instructions for A-Line Skirt, Fitted Waist. (*See page* 19.) Determine the length of skirt you want, then add ½" for the waistline and 1" for the hem. *Reminder:* You can use a tape measure or yardstick to mark the hemline in several places, following the curve of the waistline. Connect the dots and draw the curved line for the hem.

3. Cut two identical pieces, one for the front and one for the back. To cut a facing for the skirt, use the skirt pattern piece as a guide. (*See page* 37.) The facing should be about 3" wide and match the shape of the skirt. Cut two pieces (a front and a back).

HOW DOES IT LOOK?

It's smart to try on your skirt after you stitch the side seams, to adjust the fit. You can make the waistline bigger by trimming ⅛" off the top edge of the fabric. Careful, a little bit of trimming goes a long way! If the skirt is too big, turn it inside out and pin along the side seams until it fits. Stitch new side seams along the pin line. (Also, read about darts on page 27.)

If you do trim the waist or adjust the side seams, make sure the facing pieces still fit the skirt. If necessary, cut new facings. If the skirt is too long, cut off what you don't want — but remember to leave 1" for turning under the hem.

PUT IT TOGETHER

1. *Seam prep.* Staystitch the waist edge of the two skirt pieces and the facing pieces. With right sides together, use a basting stitch to sew the left-hand side seam from the waist edge to 7" below the waistline. After 7", change the stitch length to normal, backtack, and stitch the seam all the way to the hemline. Finish the seam edges and press open.

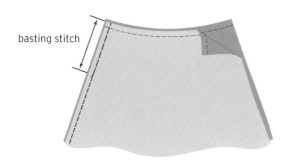

basting stitch

2. *Zipper.* Take a deep breath. Relax. Now, put in your zipper. (*See pages* 39–40.)

3. *Side seams.* With right sides together, use a normal stitch to sew the right-hand side seam. Then, before you go any further, try on the skirt. After making adjustments, finish the seam edges and press the seam open.

4. *Facing.* Next, sew on the facing, turning the ends under to clear the zipper. Hand-sew in place. (*See pages* 37–39.)

5. *Hem.* Make a ½" double-fold hem on the bottom of the skirt. (*See page* 28.)

6. *Buttons.* Sew on buttons wherever you like.

psssl...

OFF THE HiP

It's popular these days to wear skirts lower than your natural waistline. Decide where you want the top of your skirt to be and measure that spot to use as your waist measurement. Pattern manufacturers assume that the widest part of the hips is 8" below the waist. This may not be true for you. The widest part of your body may be 2" or 10" below your waist. Once you've figured out your fitting preferences, apply that formula to every skirt you make.

Tourist Trap

This skirt was made using a vintage souvenir tablecloth from Florida. Any skirt you make is one-of-a-kind, but you are generally using fabric available to anyone else who shops at the same store. A cotton or linen tablecloth about 50" wide (or more) can offer unique possibilities for a skirt no one else will be wearing. This skirt has a zipper in the back, with a waistline facing and custom pockets.

Stuff You Need

Vintage tablecloth about 50" wide, or 1½ yards of fabric with a border print

1 spool of matching or contrasting thread

1 matching 7"–9" skirt zipper

Iron-on interfacing (optional)

2 decorative buttons (optional)

Basting glue or tape (optional)

½"-wide clear tape (optional)

What You'll Do

Draft the pattern

Cut out the skirt

Put in the zipper

Pockets with buttons

Straight seams

Waistline facing

Double-fold hem

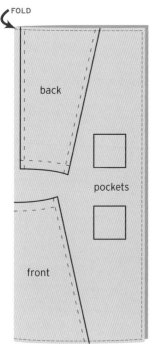

FOLD

back

pockets

front

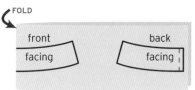

FOLD

front
facing

back
facing

LAY IT OUT, CUT IT UP

1. Prepare the fabric, then lay it out smooth on a cutting surface. (*See page* 13.)

2. For this skirt, it is especially helpful to make a paper pattern first; move it around on the tablecloth to plan where to cut the printed design. Refer to chapter 1 for drafting a pattern to fit your size. Follow the instructions for A-Line Skirt, Fitted Waist. (*See page* 19.) *Reminder:* When you have a back zipper, the back is cut in half and sewn up the middle. You need to add 1" to the width of the back pieces, for two ½" seam allowances.

Determine the length of skirt you want, then add ½" for the waistline and 1" for the hem. *Note:* If your hem lines up with the finished edge of the tablecloth, you won't need to hem it and can skip the extra 1". Don't curve the hemline edge in this case, but leave it straight along the tablecloth edge.

3. The size and shape of the pockets is up to you. Ours were made from four rectangles approximately 6"x 6". Two of the rectangles are for the lining of the pockets, which will show. Picture this when you decide where to cut out your pockets.

4. To cut a waistline facing, use the skirt pattern pieces as a guide. (*See page* 37.) The facing should be about 3" wide and match the shape of the skirt. Cut three pieces (one for the front, two halves for the back). If the tablecloth is a heavier fabric or there isn't enough, make the facing out of a different fabric.

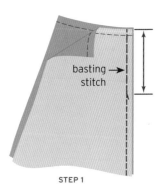

basting →
stitch

STEP 1

PUT IT TOGETHER

1. *Seam prep.* Staystitch the waistline edge of the three skirt pieces and the three facing pieces. Put the two back pieces right sides together and use a basting stitch from the waist edge to 7" below the waistline. After 7", change the stitch length to normal, backtack, and sew the seam all the way to the hemline. Finish the seam edges and press the seam allowances open.

2. *Zipper.* See pages 39–40 for how to put in your zipper.

3. *Pockets.* These pockets are made like the ones on page 46, but in a different shape. With right sides together and using a ¼" seam, sew two pocket pieces together, leaving an inch or two open at the bottom for turning. Clip off the corners where the top meets the side. Turn the pocket right side out, and gently push out the seams with a chopstick. Make two.

Fold back one corner on each pocket and sew on a button. Pin both pockets to the skirt. How far down? Hold the front skirt piece against your body and see where your arms naturally fall. Start at one folded corner, backtack, and then stitch around to the other folded corner and backtack again. Stitch a second row ¼" away.

4. *Side seams.* With right sides together, use a normal stitch for the side seams. Then try on the skirt. After making adjustments, finish the seam edges, and press open.

5. *Facing.* Next, sew on the facing. (*See pages* 37–39.)

6. *Hem.* Depending on how you cut the skirt, you might have a finished tablecloth edge along the bottom, in which case there is no need to hem this skirt. Otherwise, make a ½" double-fold hem. (*See page* 28.)

top stitching

CREATIVE LAYOUT

Depending on the size of your tablecloth, you may have another layout option. By placing the back pieces sideways along the edge, you can incorporate the border into an interesting design on the back of the skirt.

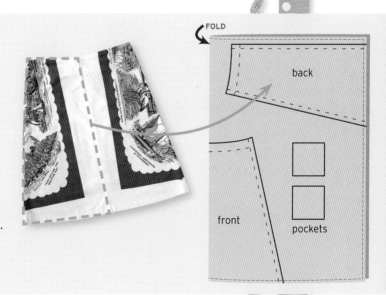

FOLD

back

front

pockets

*W*RAPAROUND CLOTHING has been in fashion off and on since the beginning of time. Before zippers, buttons, and snaps, before the invention of the needle, the easiest way to cover the body was to wrap up in an animal skin or a piece of cloth. The Roman toga, the Indian sari, and the Scottish great kilt are all variations of this approach.

Today's wraparounds are easy to put on and take off, easy to make, and forgiving if we add or lose a pound here and there. In this chapter, we describe how to make two different wraparounds: a short A-line skirt with a tie at the waist and a longer skirt held together with snap tape. The first one opens in the back, and the second opens in the front.

5 Wrap It!

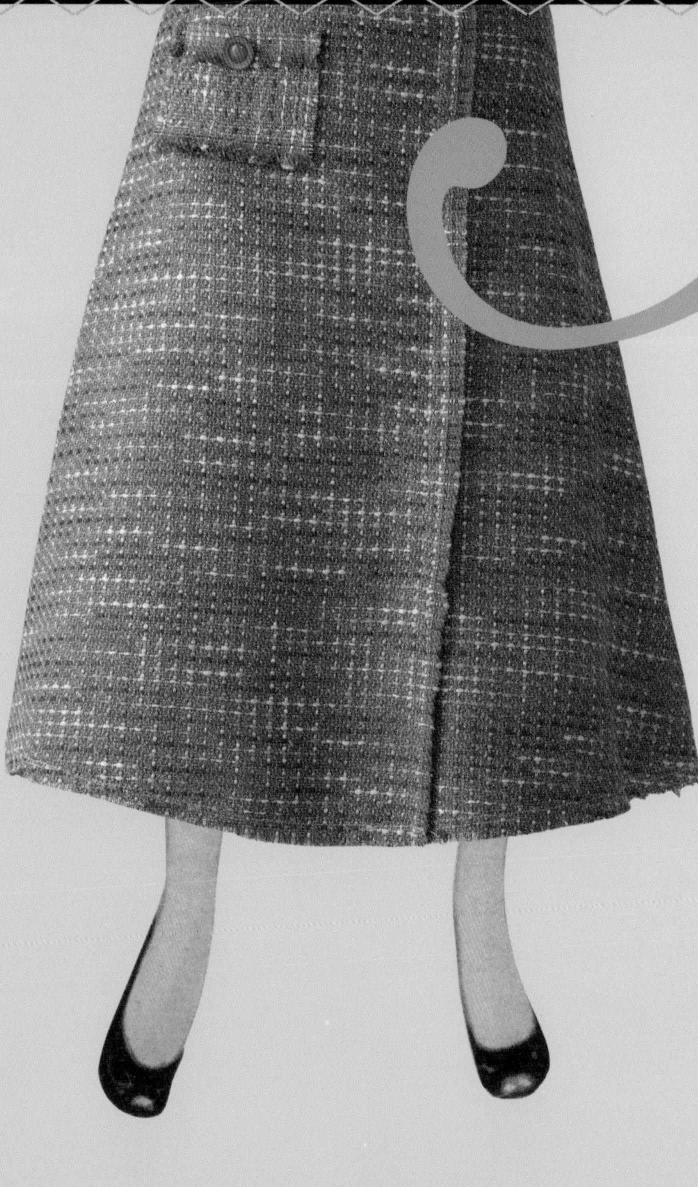

Breezy Beach Wrap

For this easy wrap, we used a cheery lightweight cotton, perfect for going to the beach. It opens in the back, ties in the front, and has an optional buttonhole on one side for the tie to go through. The shape is based on the A-line skirt, except the back has two pieces that overlap. Got suntan lotion?

Stuff You Need

1½–2 yards of 42"–45" fabric

1 spool of contrasting or matching thread

What You'll Do

Draft the pattern

Cut out the skirt

Straight seams

Waistband and ties

Optional buttonhole

Double-fold hem

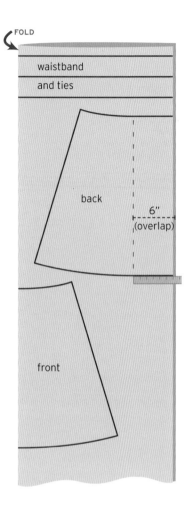

FOLD

waistband
and ties

back

6"
(overlap)

front

LAY IT OUT, CUT IT UP

1. Prepare the fabric, then lay it out smooth on a cutting surface. (*See page* 13.) Notice the direction of the nap or pattern design.

2. *Front piece.* Refer to chapter 1 for drafting a pattern to fit your size. Follow the instructions for A-Line Skirt, Fitted Waist. (*See page* 19.) Determine the length of skirt you want, then add ½" for the waistline seam allowance and 1" for the hem. Cut out the front piece.

3. *Back panels.* Take the folded front piece you've just cut out (or the paper pattern you've made) and flip it over. Line up the folded edge with the selvage, but move it 6" away. To make sure it's straight, measure 6" at both the waist and the bottom of the panel. The extra 6" creates the overlap in the back.

With chalk and a ruler, draw straight lines from the selvage to the front piece, one at the waistline and one at the hemline, then trace around the edge of the front panel. Cut along the chalk lines through both layers of fabric.

4. *Waistband and ties.* Cut two strips on the horizontal grainline (at a right angle from selvage to selvage) that are 3" wide (they will be 42"–45" long, the width of your fabric). This will produce a waistband that is 1" wide when folded in half and sewn. If you want a wider or narrower waistband, adjust the width accordingly.

PUT IT TOGETHER

1. *Side seams.* Pin the back pieces (the nonselvage edges) along the side seams of the front piece, one on each side, right sides together. Stitch from the bottom to the top. Finish the seam edges and press open the seam allowances. Along the outside edges of the back panels, finish with a double-fold hem. (*See page* 28.)

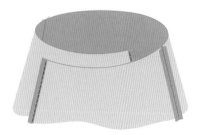

2. *Waistband and ties.* With right sides together, stitch the two waistband pieces into one long strip. Press the seam open. With right sides together, center this seam at the middle of the front piece (where it was folded). Pin the waistband tie all along the waistline edge of the skirt, then stitch a ½" seam.

center

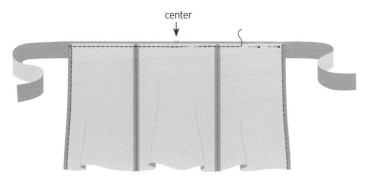

Press the waistband and both seam allowances toward the waistband. Now fold the waistband in half, right sides together, and pin the ties all the way to the ends. On both ties, stitch a ½" seam from the end of the tie exactly to the waistline edge of the skirt. Do not stitch over the skirt piece. Clip the corners on the ends of the ties.

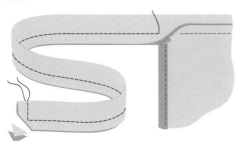

Use a long chopstick or dowel to push the fabric right side out, then press the ties flat.

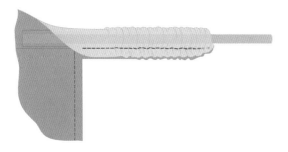

Fold under the raw edge of the waistband just short of a ½", press, and pin it to the waistline seam. Finish the waistband using the stitch-in-the-ditch technique described in chapter 2. (*See page* 36.)

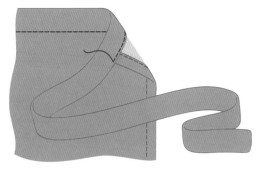

3. *Optional buttonhole.* You can just tie the skirt around your waist and be done with it. However, if you want a tidier, more secure waistline, you can make a buttonhole for the ties. Use the directions that came with your sewing machine and make a vertical buttonhole in the waistband above the left seam.

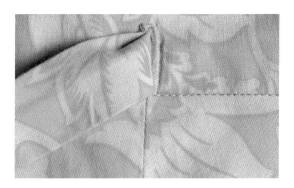

4. *Hem.* To finish the skirt, make a ½" double-fold hem. (*See page* 28.) Remember that the bobbin stitches will show. Choose your thread accordingly.

Half-Circle Wrap

For another great wrap idea, the skirt pictured here is a variation of the circle skirt featured on pages 76–79. However, you need only a half circle, so it uses less fabric. And it has all the great features of a wrap — no side seams, zippers, or buttons to mess with. A buttonhole is optional. All you need is 2 lengths of 42"–45" fabric plus ⅛ yard for the waistband and ties. Here's what you do:

1. *Cutting out the skirt.* Follow directions on page 78 for preparing, measuring, and cutting the fabric, with two exceptions:

- Cut only one half circle instead of two.

- You will need to add to the **W** measurement to allow for fabric overlap in the back of the skirt. To do this, measure where your waistline will be, then add 12" to 14" (or the amount you want it to overlap). Divide by 6 and round up to the nearest ½". Then make your string compass as instructed.

2. *Cutting out the ties.* Follow directions on page 62.

3. *Side seams.* Stitch a ½" double-fold hem on the straight edges of the half circle. (*See page* 28.)

4. *Hem.* Stitch a ¼" hem along the curved edge. (*See sidebar on page* 79.)

5. *Waistband and ties.* The directions are the same as for the *Breezy Beach Wrap*. (*See page* 63.)

6. *Optional buttonhole.* Make one if you want a flatter, smoother waistline effect. (*See pages* 41 *and* 64.)

Got No Ties

A loosely woven fabric is an ideal choice for making fringed hems — not only along the bottom, but also along the front panel edges and waistline. This super-easy wrap has no ties to worry about, and snap tape makes the front opening, well, pretty much a snap. The cut of the skirt is slightly A-line, with two side seams. An easy fringed pocket with a button adds the final touch of style.

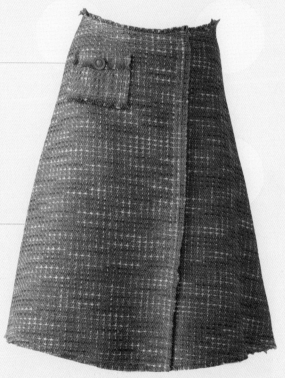

Stuff You Need

2 lengths* of 42"–45" bouclé or other loosely woven fabric

1 spool of contrasting or matching thread

²/₃ yard of snap tape

1 decorative button

What You'll Do

Draft the pattern

Cut out the skirt

Straight seams

Fringed edges and hem

Snap tape

Pockets

Sew on the button

*Measure the distance from your waist to the desired hemline and add a couple of inches.

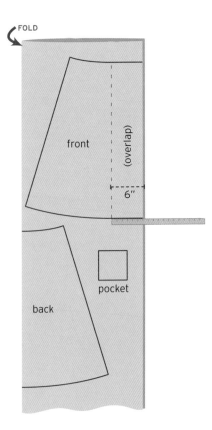

front

(overlap)

6"

pocket

back

LAY IT OUT, CUT IT UP

1. Prepare the fabric according to the directions on the bolt, then lay it out smooth on a cutting surface. (*See page* 13.) Notice the direction of the nap or pattern design.

2. *Back piece.* Refer to chapter 1 for drafting a pattern to fit your size. Follow the instructions for A-Line Skirt, Fitted Waist. (*See page* 19.) (Because all edges are fringed, you don't need to add any seam allowances.) Cut out this piece.

3. *Front panels.* Take the folded back piece you've just cut out (or the paper pattern you've made) and flip it over. Line up the folded edge with the selvage, but move it 6" away. To make sure it's straight, measure 6" at both the waist and the bottom of the panel. With chalk and a ruler, draw straight lines from the selvage to the front piece, one at the waistline and one at the hemline, then trace around the edge of the front panel. Cut out the two front panels.

4. *Pocket.* If you want a fringed pocket, cut a square on the straight of the grain. Ours is 5½" x 5½".

DON'T WANT FRINGE?

If you choose cotton or some other tightly woven fabric, a fringed hem won't work. In that case, finish the bottom and side edges with a double-fold hem. The waistline edge can be finished with a facing (*see pages* 37–39) or seam binding (*see Taped Hem, page* 29). For a dressier look, you can always shop for a special trim (maybe lace, maybe ribbon?) to attach to the hem and front edges.

PUT IT TOGETHER

1. *Side seams.* Pin the front pieces (the nonselvage edges) to the back piece along the side seams, right sides together. Stitch from the bottom to the top. Because this is a bulkier fabric that unravels easily, finish the seams by pressing them open, then stitching them to the skirt pieces with a zigzag stitch. These stitches will show on either side of both side seams.

Try on the skirt. Overlap the front panels (right over left), and pin them in place. Are the side seams in the right place? If your back piece is too big or too small, adjust the side seams now.

2. *Fringe.* Follow instructions on page 29 for making a fringed hem. You can zigzag and fringe the edges all the way around.

3. *Snap tape.* The snap tape will run in a straight line from your waist as far down as you want. How much leg do you want to show? Cut the length of snap tape to the desired length.

Unsnap the tape. One side has snap bumps and the other side has holes. With pins, basting glue, or basting tape, attach the side with the snap holes along the inside edge of your top panel, away from the fringe. Start at the waistline and run straight down the selvage line. Sew the tape in place by stitching close to the edge of the tape around all sides. You might need to use a zipper foot.

Snap both sides of the tape together and put on the skirt. Adjust the fit and make sure the top and hem edges are even, then start pinning. Pin the top, middle, and bottom edges of the snap tape (the side with the bumps) where you want it to go. Carefully unsnap the tape and pin or glue it more securely, then sew it to the skirt. Add an extra snap or two as needed on the inner part of the panel (*see photo*).

4. *Pocket.* A fringed pocket is the simplest thing imaginable. Just turn over the top edge and stitch a zigzag or two across the flap before fringing. Then figure out where you want the pocket and topstitch it on! Backtack at the beginning and end of the stitches. Add a button, if you wish.

STEP 3

STEP 4

*Y*OU CAN MAKE A SKIRT out of almost anything, and you can start with any number of shapes. Rectangles, squares, and circles are the most popular and the easiest to adapt. In chapter 4, we converted a square tablecloth into a modified A-line skirt. In this chapter, we use a square and a circle without much modification. No need to draft a pattern for these skirts — the key is in the way you fold and cut the fabric.

For our *Short and Sassy* skirt we used a square piece of fabric, but a nice square tablecloth, about 60" x 60", would work just as well. For the circle skirt, we cut out two half circles from fabric and stitched them together. If you come across a circular tablecloth with enough yardage to be long enough for you, give it a try. You are limited only by your imagination.

6

Circles & Squares

Short and Sassy

If you have nice legs and like to show them off, this skirt's for you! The irregular hem-line might look hard to make, but in truth it's very simple. The whole skirt is cut from one big square, with a hole in the middle for the waist. Shy people beware: the sides of this skirt will be less than half the width of the fabric. Since most fabrics are about 45" wide, your shortest sides will be about 18" long.

Stuff You Need

Enough fabric (we suggest rayon or a lightweight tablecloth) to make a 45"–60" square

1 spool of contrasting or matching thread

1 package of ⅞"-wide double-fold bias tape

1 yard of ¾" non-roll elastic

What You'll Do

Measure the square

Cut the waistline hole

Double-fold hem

Bias-tape waistline casing

Put in the elastic

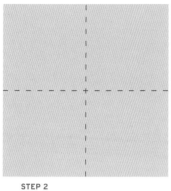

STEP 2

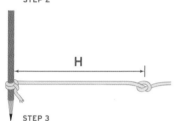

H

STEP 3

FOLD

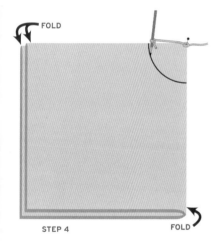

STEP 4   FOLD

LAY IT OUT, CUT IT UP

1. Prepare the fabric as instructed on the bolt. (*See page* 13.) Then, make the largest square you can from your fabric. This will be determined by its width — most likely you'll have a 45" x 45" square. If you have 60"-wide fabric, measure and cut a 60" x 60" square. Square vintage tablecloths come in all sizes; ideally, you want something square from 50"–70" wide.

2. Fold the fabric in half lengthwise and then widthwise.

3. Measure your hips and divide by 6. We'll call this measurement **H**. This is an approximation, so it's okay to round up to the nearest ½". Find a piece of string without much stretch. Tie your chalk marker at one end of the string. Tie a knot at a distance equal to the **H** measurement.

4. Put a pin through the knot and into the folded corner of the fabric. Draw an arc from fold to fold, using the chalk and string as a compass.

5. Cut the fabric on the chalk line. When you open up the folded fabric, you will have a circular hole in the middle of a square. Try this on over your hips. If you can't easily pull the skirt over your hips, very carefully cut off no more than ¹⁄₁₆" around the waist edge and try again. (*See sidebar at right.*) It is better to cut off too little than too much; cut off very small amounts until you can pull the skirt over your hips.

ViTAL STATiSTiCS

For this pattern, you will need this measurement.

H = Your hips ÷ 6 = _____

PUT IT TOGETHER

1. *Hem.* If you are using a finished tablecloth, your hem is already done. Otherwise, make a ¼" double-fold hem on each of the four sides of the fabric. (*See page* 28.) If you have a very clean selvage, you may need only a single-fold hem on the selvage edges.

2. *Waistline casing.* Staystitch the waistline edge and clip. (*See page* 26.) Cut a piece of double-fold bias tape the same length as the top of the skirt, plus 1". Attach the bias tape to the top of the skirt, as shown on page 34. Remember to keep the narrower fold of the tape on the right side (outside) of the skirt. The skirt front and back are the same, so it doesn't matter where you start.

3. *Elastic.* Cut a piece of ¾" elastic to fit your waist, plus a 1" overlap. Use a large safety pin to thread the elastic through the bias-tape waistband. Take care not to let the elastic twist or roll over — you want the elastic to lie flat in the casing. Overlap and pin the ends of the elastic together and try on the skirt. Adjust the tightness of the elastic and repin. Securely sew the two ends of the elastic together and close the opening of the bias tape with a slipstitch. (*See page* 33.)

FINE-TUNING THE WAISTLINE

If your waist opening is too small, there is more than one way to fix it. If you have a steady hand, you can trim off ¹⁄₁₆" all around the waistline edge. Or, fold the skirt in half so the waist opening is a semicircle, and carefully trim off ¹⁄₁₆" just on the folds on each side. The key: don't take off too much the first time. It will astound you to see how much larger the circle opening will become with even the merest ¹⁄₁₆" removed.

'Tis the Season

If you like long flowing skirts with lots of fabric, this elegant holiday skirt is just perfect for dancing the night away. This skirt is essentially two half circles cut from lightweight, embroidered silk and sewn together. A glittery rickrack trim at the waist adds a final touch of sparkle. You can use almost any lightweight fabric for your skirt, but avoid striped, directional, or border prints.

Stuff You Need

Approximately 5⅛ yards of 42"–45" of fabric

1 spool of matching thread

1 matching 7"–9" skirt zipper

1 package of glittery rickrack

1 button

Interfacing for waistband (optional)

½"-wide clear tape (optional)

What You'll Do

Cut out the skirt and waistband

Straight seams

Put in the zipper

Attach the waistband

Make a buttonhole

Sew on a button

Add trim

Double-fold hem

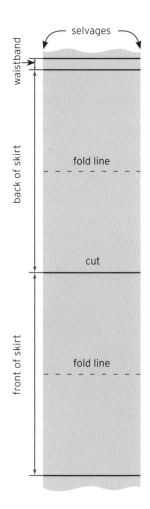

LAY IT OUT, CUT IT UP

1. Prepare the fabric per the instructions on the bolt. (*See page 13.*) Cut out the waistband first, from selvage to selvage. This skirt has a 2"-wide waistband, folded over (+2"), plus two seam allowances (+1"), which equals 5". Therefore, the waistband strip is 5" x 45" (probably more length than you need; you can cut it to fit later).

2. After you cut out the waistband, cut the rest of the fabric in half (fold it lengthwise to find the halfway point). You should have two rectangles about 2½ yards long. Fold each rectangle in half to make a square about 42" (1¼ yards) on each side. Trim as needed to even up the square.

3. Measure your waist (or where you want the skirt to ride) and divide by 6. We'll call this measurement **W**. This is an approximation, so it's okay to round up to the nearest ½". Decide how long you want the skirt, and add 1½" for seam allowance and hem (the total can be no longer than the width of the fabric). This will be measurement **L**.

4. Find a piece of string as long as the length of your skirt, plus about 10". Tie your chalk marker at one end of the string. From the chalk, measure up the length of **W** and tie a knot. From that knot, measure up the length of **L** and make a second knot.

5. For the waistline, pin the knot closest to the chalk on the folded corner of the fabric. With the chalk end, draw an arc.

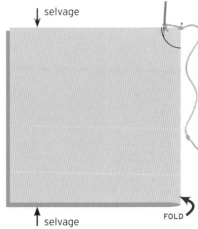

6. Move the pin to the second knot and once more pin the rope on the folded corner. Draw the hemline arc. Check the **L** measurement with a yardstick, from waist to hemline, at several points along the arc.

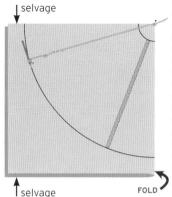

selvage

selvage   FOLD

7. Cut on the chalk lines, but do not unfold this piece yet. Use it to cut another identical piece from the second rectangle. Now you can open them up. You should be looking at two big half circles — one for the skirt front, one for the back.

PUT IT TOGETHER

1. *Side seams and zipper.* Put the right sides together, then prepare the seam and install a zipper. (*See pages 39–40.*) *Note:* Basting glue is not recommended for silk. Next, stitch the other side seam. Press the seams open and finish the raw edges.

2. *Prepare the curve.* Since you will be sewing a curved edge (the skirt waistline) to a straight edge (the waistband), follow the directions on page 26 for sewing a curved edge.

3. *Waistband.* Take your waist measurement, then add 2" for waistband overlap and 1" for two seam allowances. Cut the waistband to this length. See the instructions on pages 36–37 for putting in an attached waistband.

4. *Buttonhole.* Make a horizontal buttonhole where the ends of the waistband overlap. The buttonhole goes where the top flap overlaps; sew the button on the underlap. (*See page* 41.)

5. *Rickrack.* Sew the trim on top of the waistband seam, turning under both ends.

6. *Hem.* Very carefully, make a ¼" double-fold hem on the bottom of the skirt. (*See sidebar.*)

OBSTiNATE HEMS

Sewing a curved hem can be tricky. The fabric doesn't fold easily on the curve and could get all puckered. Three possible solutions are:

1. Make the folded hem even narrower than ¼". The less fabric you have to turn, the better.

2. Make a single-fold hem using a basting stitch. Then, while turning over the second fold, gently pull on the basting stitches, to ease in the extra fabric.

3. Apply trim to the bottom edge. Then you only have to make a single-fold hem and cover the raw edge with the trim.

Check out the Half-Circle Wrap on page 65!

A FITTED STRAIGHT SKIRT will hug your body line along the waist and hips, then run straight down on each side — a great choice for showing off a trim body. To walk comfortably in a straight skirt, especially a long one, you need a slit along the sides or in the back.

Once you know how to make a fitted straight skirt, then the fun begins. You might decide to make a fitted top (or yoke), then add something different at the bottom — a pleated panel, for instance. With pleats, you won't need a slit. How much fullness you put in the pleats is up to you. They can be wide or narrow, just in the front, or all the way around. They may be evenly or irregularly spaced. You are the designer. Step out of the box and have fun with your new creation.

Play It Straight
with Flair

7

Polka Dotty

For a dash of fun, try something like this polished cotton fabric with polka dots, two side seams, a side zipper, and a facing. With fabric this lively, who needs embellishments? The length of the skirt and the easy-to-make side slits are up to you. Just how daring do you want to be?

Stuff You Need

1 length* of 45" fabric if your hips are less than 42" (otherwise, 2 lengths)

1 spool of all-purpose thread

1 matching 7"–9" skirt zipper

Iron-on interfacing (optional)

Basting glue or tape (optional)

½"-wide clear tape (optional)

What You'll Do

Draft the pattern

Cut out the skirt

Put in the zipper

Straight seams

Waistline facing

Side slits

Double-fold hem

Measure the distance from your waist to the desired hemline and add a couple of inches.

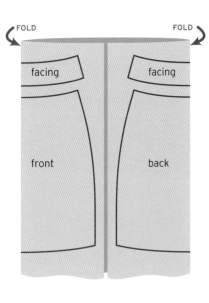

FOLD   FOLD

facing   facing

front   back

LAY IT OUT, CUT IT UP

1. Prepare the fabric as instructed on the bolt. (*See page* 13.) Notice the direction of the nap or pattern design. If your hips are less than 42", you can cut this skirt out of a yard or less of fabric. See the layout diagram at left for how to make two folds and arrange your pieces.

2. See chapter 1 for drafting a pattern to fit your size. Follow the instructions for Straight Skirt, Fitted Waist. (*See page* 18.) Determine the length of skirt you want, then add 1" for the hem and ½" for the waistline seam allowance.

3. Cut two identical pieces, one for the front and one for the back. To cut a facing for the skirt, use the skirt pattern piece as a guide. The facing should be about 3" wide and match the shape of the skirt. Cut two pieces. (*See pages 37–39.*)

FiTTiNG ADViCE

For your first attempt at a straight skirt, cut the pieces an inch or two larger than your measurements dictate. After you put in the zipper and side seams, turn the skirt inside out and put it on. Pin along the side seams to get a perfect fit. (Also, read about darts on page 27.) Mark the pin line with chalk, remove the pins, and stitch new side seams. One you've got it right, make a pattern for your next skirt, and the rest is easy.

PUT IT TOGETHER

1. *Plan the slits.* Decide how long you want your side slits to be. You can do this by holding a skirt piece against your body and marking with a pin how high you want the slit to go. (Our skirt is 20½" long, with a 6"-long slit.) If you want a 6" slit, add 1" for a double-fold hem and place your pin 7" up from the bottom. Place a second pin on the other side of the same skirt piece to mark the slit in the other side.

2. *Zipper.* Follow the steps in chapter 3 for putting in a zipper, except you start stitching the left-hand seam from the spot where you put the pin for the slit. (*See pages 39–40.*)

3. *Side seam.* Stitch the right-hand seam, starting from the spot where you put the second pin. Try on the skirt and make any necessary adjustments. When you're satisfied with the fit, finish the seam edges and press open.

4. *Facing.* Prepare and attach the facing. (*See pages 37–39.*)

facing

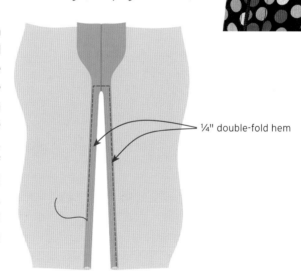

5. *Finish the slits.* For each slit, make a ¼" double-fold hem from the bottom of the hemline to about ¼" above where the seam is sewn together. Leave the needle in place and turn the fabric, then stitch across the top of the slit. Backtack across and back to reinforce the seam. Turn the other corner and sew a ¼" double-fold hem on the other side.

¼" double-fold hem

6. *Hem.* Finish the bottom with a ¼" double-fold hem. (*See page 28.*)

Wine and Dine

The look is fancy, but the sewing is easy. This long, straight skirt is cut from a shiny prequilted fabric, with a short panel of elegant novelty fabric in front. Bias tape forms a thin waistband; the zipper and a generous slit are sewn into the back seam.

Stuff You Need

1 length* of 45" fabric if your hips are less than 42" (otherwise, 2 lengths)

1 spool of contrasting or matching thread

¼ yard of contrasting fabric for overlay

1 matching 7"–9" skirt zipper

1 package of ½" double-fold bias tape

½"-wide clear tape (optional)

What You'll Do

Draft the pattern

Cut out the skirt

Baste the overlay piece

Put in the zipper

Straight seams

Bias-tape waistband

Back slit

Double-fold hem

Measure the distance from your waist to the desired hemline and add a couple of inches.

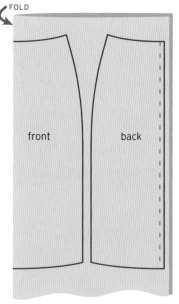

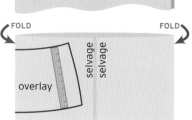

LAY IT OUT, CUT IT UP

1. Prepare the fabric according to the instructions on the bolt. (*See page* 13.) Notice the direction of the nap or pattern design. If your hip size plus seam allowance plus ease is less than 45", you can cut the main skirt out of one length of fabric. (*See the diagram at left.*)

2. See chapter 1 for drafting a pattern to fit your size. Follow the instructions for Straight Skirt, Fitted Waist. (*See page 18.*) Determine the length of skirt you want, then add 1½". (Ours is 32", which includes the hem and seam allowance.)

3. Cut out three pieces from the main fabric: one front piece on the fold, and two back pieces on the selvage. *Reminder:* Add ½" to each back piece for seam allowance. Use the front piece as a pattern for the front overlay panel. This piece can be whatever length you like (ours is 9½"); add ½" for the waist seam allowance and 1" for a double-fold hem. Use a ruler to check that the length is consistent all across the piece.

CUTOUT CLUES

Here are a few pointers for cutting out this skirt:

- Only the front needs to be cut on the fold, because the back will have a seam up the middle.

- When laying out the back pieces, move them about an inch away from the edge of the fabric so you won't have selvages in your seams.

- The front panel is cut from a second fabric. Fold it so that the selvages meet in the center. This way you save a larger piece of fabric to use for another project.

PUT IT TOGETHER

1. *Overlay fabric.* Make a ¼" double-fold hem across the bottom of the overlay fabric and press the edge. Position the overlay fabric on top of the skirt front, right side up. Use a basting stitch to attach the overlay to the front on both sides and along the top edge. The skirt front can now be treated as one piece.

2. *Plan the slits.* Decide how long you want your back slit to be. To make it easier to walk, it will help if the top of the slit is above where your knees bend. Mark the spot with a pin on one of the back piece's seam allowances.

3. *Zipper.* Follow the steps in chapter 3 for putting in a zipper, except you start sewing the seam from the spot where you put the pin. (*See pages* 39–40.)

4. *Side seams.* Sew the side seams together. Before you finish the waistline, try on the skirt. Adjust the side seams if needed to make your skirt fit the way you like it. Because it doesn't ravel much, this fabric can be finished nicely with just pinking. Press the seams open or to one side.

5. *Bias-tape waistband.* Attach the ½" double-fold bias tape at the waistline. (*See page* 35.)

6. *Back slit.* Try on the skirt again and adjust the length of the skirt. If it is too long, mark with pins the length you prefer. Then adjust the length of the back slit. Sew a ¼" double-fold hem on either side of the slit. (*See page* 85.)

7. *Hem.* Finish with a ½" double-fold hem. (*See page* 28.)

SLiT HiGH, SLiT LOW

When you get to step 6, walk around in your skirt. Is the back slit long enough? Too long? If you want to change it, mark with a pin where you want the top of the slit to be.

If the slit is too long, turn the skirt inside out and extend the back middle seam by stitching down to where you marked with a pin. If the slit is too short, stitch and backtack above the pin, then rip out the unwanted portion of the middle seam.

Asian Dream

The top of a straight skirt, cut short, can serve as a yoke for all kinds of bottom treatments. Pleats are easy to make and can be any length or width. If you don't like pleats, make ruffles instead (*see pages* 114–115). A different-color bottom fabric or a special trim can make all the difference. This skirt has a back zipper.

Stuff You Need

Approximately 2 yards of 42"–45" fabric

1 spool of contrasting or matching thread

1 matching 7"–9" skirt zipper

Iron-on interfacing (optional)

Ribbon or trim (optional)

Basting glue or tape (optional)

½"-wide clear tape (optional)

What You'll Do

Draft the pattern

Cut out the skirt

Make the pleats

Put in the zipper

Straight seams

Waistline facing

Add trim (optional)

Double-fold hem

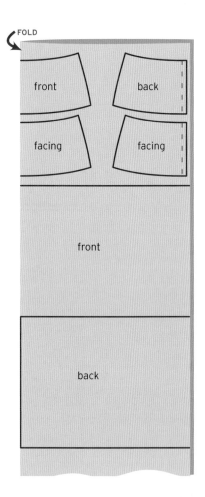

LAY IT OUT, CUT IT UP

1. Prepare the fabric as instructed on the bolt, then lay it out smooth on a cutting surface. (*See page* 13.) Notice the direction of the nap or pattern design.

2. See chapter 1 for drafting a pattern to fit your size. For this skirt, it's best to draft the pattern on paper, then use it to draw the yoke. Follow the instructions for Straight Skirt, Fitted Waist. (*See page* 18.) Decide how long you want the yoke to be (ours is 6"), then add 1" for two seam allowances.

3. Cut the front yoke on the fold, and another the same size for the facing. Cut the back yoke pieces along the selvage, about an inch away from the edges. Don't forget to add ½" to each back edge for the seam allowance. Cut two more the same size for the facing. (*See page* 37.)

4. For the pleated panels, decide how long you want them to be (ours are 16"), then add 1½" for the top seam allowance and hem. Cut both panels on the fold, then cut *one* of the panels in half to make two pieces for the back.

KiNKY CREASES

How many pleats and how much fullness the skirt has is up to you. We suggest making the pleats by trial and error, rather than following some mathematical formula. For fun and practice, lay out the front panel and fold it different ways. Find the look you like.

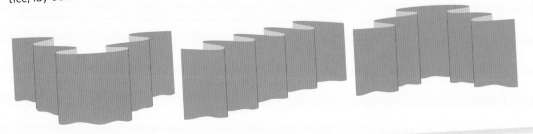

PUT IT TOGETHER

1. *Pleats.* Pin the pleated front panel to the front yoke piece, right sides together. First adjust the pleats until the width of the panel matches the bottom width of the yoke, then stitch a ½" seam. Press the seams up toward the waist edge. Do the same for the two back panels and yoke pieces. The folds of the back pleats don't have to match the front — it's your call.

2. *Zipper.* Put the two back pieces right sides together and follow the instructions in chapter 3 for putting in a zipper. (*See pages* 39–40.)

3. *Side seams.* Sew the side seams together. Before you finish the waistline, try on the skirt. Adjust the side seams if needed (with your skirt inside out) to make your skirt fit the way you like it. Finish the seam edges, and press the seams open.

4. *Facing.* Prepare and attach the facing. Lighter fabrics might need stiffening to hold the waistline edge; if so, use iron-on interfacing. (*See pages* 37–39.) Understitch or topstitch the facing.

5. *Trim.* The right trim can really make the skirt. Measure the length you need to go all the way around the yoke seam, adding ½" –1" for the ends. Tuck the ends under on either side of the zipper, and stitch the ends, top edge, and bottom edge of the trim.

6. *Hem.* Finish the bottom with a ½" double-fold hem. (*See page* 28.)

SAME iDEA, DiFFERENT RESULT

Can you believe it? The skirt below is made using the same basic steps as *Asian Dream*. The fabric and trim are different, the yoke is longer, and the pleated section has less fabric with only two pleats. This version — with a side zipper, bias-tape waistband, and fewer pieces to cut — is easier to make. Notice that we matched the stripes on the top piece to the stripes on the bottom piece.

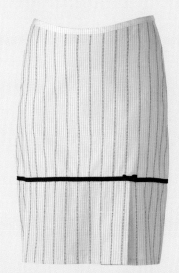

ONCE YOU KNOW how to make the basic shapes and styles presented so far, you can really take it to the next level. Layering fabrics is a lot of fun, and there are many ways to go about it. To get your ideas flowing, we show you three options in this chapter.

The underskirt of the *Barbie's Dream Skirt* is essentially a long A-line shape, with a sheer "apron" of the same length put on backward (with the ties in the front). *Country Charm* is made with two complementary fabrics, cut as two A-lines, and sewn together. The top layer is cut shorter, to show off the fabric underneath. *Chinese Takeout* features a dramatic fabric underneath, with a sheer, dotted tulle on top that extends below the hemline. The possibilities are endless!

Layer It! 8

Barbie's Dream Skirt

Bubble-gum pink fades to peach beneath a sheer golden layer of spotted organza — enough to brighten any after-dark activity. The underskirt is an A-line with a bias-tape waistline facing and a side zipper. The overskirt is made like a wraparound, only easier — no side seams to bother with. It's less work to make, so there's more time to have fun!

Stuff You Need

2 lengths of 42"–45" brocade for the under-skirt plus ⅓ yard for the waistband tie

1 length of 42"–45" organza for the overskirt

1 package of ⅞" double-fold bias tape for the facing

1 spool of all-purpose thread

1 matching 7"–9" skirt zipper

What You'll Do

Draft the pattern

Cut out the skirt

Put in the zipper

Straight seams

Bias-tape waist facing

Waistband and ties

Double-fold hem

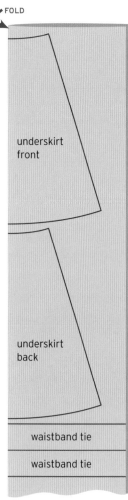

FOLD

underskirt
front

underskirt
back

waistband tie

waistband tie

FOLD

overskirt
panel

LAY IT OUT, CUT IT UP

1. Prepare the fabric according to the directions on the bolt. (*See page* 13.) Notice the direction of the nap or pattern design.

2. Refer to chapter 1 for drafting a pattern to fit your size. Follow the instructions for A-Line Skirt, Fitted Waist. (*See page* 19.) Determine the length of skirt you want, then add ½" for the waistline and 1" for the hem.

3. *Underskirt.* Cut two identical pieces, one for the front and one for the back. For the waistband ties, cut two strips of fabric 5" wide from selvage to selvage. This will produce a waistband that is 2" wide when folded in half and sewn. If you want a narrower waistband, adjust the width accordingly.

4. *Overskirt.* Cut a straight-edged rectangle that is as long as the underskirt. For the width, wrap the fabric or a tape measure around your body to decide how much overlap you want in front. Add 2" for a double-fold hem on each side, then mark and cut the fabric. (Our overskirt is 35" cut, 33" sewn.) Even though this piece is cut as a rectangle, when wrapped around your curves it will pull open along the sides to form something like an upside-down V in front.

MiX AND MATCH

In a good fabric store, you'll find several sheer options for your overskirt. Tulle or organza that isn't too slippery is probably your best bet. Pick out a favorite or two and carry the bolts around the store so you can test the effects with different fabric combinations.

PUT IT TOGETHER

Underskirt

1. *Zipper.* Put the front and back pieces right sides together and follow the steps in chapter 3 for putting in a zipper. (*See pages* 39–40.)

2. *Side seams.* With right sides together, use a normal stitch to sew the right-hand side seam. Try on the skirt. After making adjustments, finish the seam edges and press the seam open.

3. *Facing.* You can make a facing as usual (*see pages* 37–39), or try this time-saver: Use bias tape for a narrow waistline facing. Start by cutting a strip of ⅞" double-fold bias tape to the length of your waistline, plus 1". Then follow these steps:

> *a.* Press the bias tape edges flat, but leave the center fold as it is. Pin the tape to the right side of the waistline edge. Leave about ½" extra on the ends, on either side of the zipper. Backtack and stitch.

> *b.* Press the bias tape and all seams together, away from the waistline. Understitch. (*See page* 38.)

> *c.* Turn the facing to the inside of the skirt and hand-sew the ends next to the zipper. Voila!

4. *Hem.* Make a ½" double-fold hem on the bottom of the skirt. (*See page* 28.)

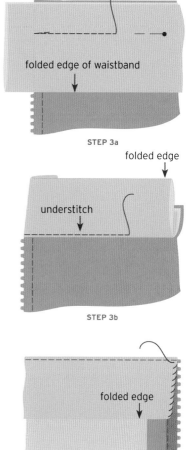

folded edge of waistband

STEP 3a

folded edge

understitch

STEP 3b

folded edge

STEP 3c

Overskirt

1. *Hem.* For once, you do the hems first! Make a ¼" double-fold hem on both sides and on the bottom of the skirt. (*See page* 28.)

2. *Waistband and ties.* Sew the ties onto the organza, following the instructions given for the *Breezy Beach Wrap*. (*See page* 63.)

3. Make yourself some dinner reservations and show off your handiwork!

overskirt waistband

bias-tape facing

overskirt waistband and tie

Country Charm

This easy-to-make charmer is simply two A-line skirts of different lengths, sewn together at the waistline. The double layers at the top make this skirt a natural for an elastic waistline casing that is easy to install. We made ours plain, but depending on the fabric you choose, you might want to add pockets or trim such as lace or rickrack.

Stuff You Need

2 lengths* of 42"–45" fabric for the underskirt

2 lengths* of 42"–45" fabric for the overskirt

1 spool of all-purpose thread

1 yard of ½" non-roll elastic

What You'll Do

Draft the pattern

Cut out the skirt

Straight seams

Waistline casing

Put in the elastic

Double-fold hem

Measure the distance from your waist to the desired hemline and add a couple of inches.

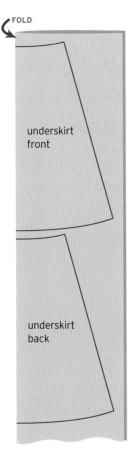

LAY IT OUT, CUT IT UP

1. Prepare the fabric as instructed on the bolt. (*See page* 13.) Notice the direction of the nap or pattern design.

2. Refer to chapter 1 for drafting a pattern to fit your size. Follow the instructions for A-Line Skirt, Elastic Waist. (*See page* 19.) *Exception:* For this kind of casing, add only ¾" to the waistline edge instead of 2". Determine the length of each skirt, then add ½" for the waistline and 1" for the hem. One nice trick for cutting this pair of skirts: Draw your side seams from the waist edge measurement all the way out to the selvage. Not only will this give your skirt extra flare, but the shorter overskirt will automatically be wider and roomier than the underskirt.

3. Cut two identical pieces for the **underskirt,** one for the front and one for the back. Cut two identical pieces for the **overskirt,** one for the front and one for the back.

FOR A GiRLiER SKiRT

It couldn't be easier to dress up this skirt. Simply stitch a lace trim to the hem of either or both layers. A simple topstitch will hold the trim in place.

PUT IT TOGETHER

1. *Side seams.* Pin and stitch both side seams for the under-skirt. Do the same for the overskirt. Finish the raw seam edges and press the seams open. Tack all seam allowances to the skirt in the casing area. (*See page* 48, *step* 4.)

2. *Waist edge seam.* Turn both skirts right side out, then put the overskirt inside the underskirt. The right side of the overskirt should be facing the wrong side of the underskirt. Stitch a ½" seam all along the top. Now pull the two pieces open like a butterfly, and press the seam open (*see illustration*). There's no need to finish the raw edges, as they will be hidden inside the elastic waistline casing.

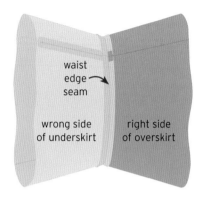

waist edge seam

wrong side of underskirt

right side of overskirt

3. *Waistline casing.* Fold the overskirt right side out, on top of the underskirt (the way the skirt will look when finished). Press along the top seam, making sure that the inner layer doesn't show on the outside. To prepare for stitching the casing, pin the two layers together along the waistline edge.

Stitch the casing through both layers along the top of the skirt so that the width of the casing matches the elastic width, plus ¼". Stop about an inch short of joining the stitching to leave a gap for inserting the elastic. (*See page* 33.)

4. *Put in the elastic.* Using a large safety pin, reach in between the two skirt layers and thread the elastic through the casing. Be care-ful not to let the elastic twist. Try on the skirt and adjust the tightness of the elastic. Stitch the ends of the elastic together. Stitch the gap closed. (*See page* 33.)

5. *Hem.* Make a ½" double-fold hem on the bottom of both skirts. (*See page* 28.)

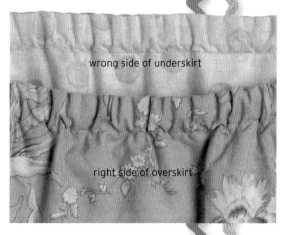

wrong side of underskirt

right side of overskirt

Chinese Takeout

Nothing says "Take me out!" like a classy evening skirt. This tempting attire is essentially two skirts, sewn together, with a bias-tape waistband and a centered back-seam zipper. The layering effect is enhanced by leaving the hemline of the tulle overskirt a couple of inches longer than the underskirt.

Stuff You Need

1 length* of 42"–45" fabric for the underskirt if your hips are less than 42" (otherwise, 2 lengths)

1–2 lengths* of dotted tulle (widths vary) for the overskirt

1 matching 7"–9" skirt zipper

1 spool of all-purpose thread

1 package of ½" double-fold bias tape

1½" ribbon or other trim (optional)

What You'll Do

Draft the pattern

Cut out the skirt

Straight seams

Put in a zipper

Bias-tape waistband

Back slit

Double-fold hem

Add trim (optional)

Measure the distance from your waist to the desired hemline and add a couple of inches.

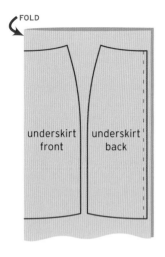

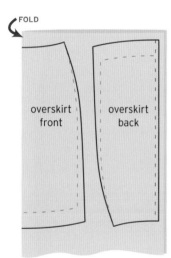

LAY IT OUT, CUT IT UP

1. *Underskirt.* Prepare the fabric according to instructions on the bolt. (*See page* 13.) Note the direction of any pattern design. If your hip size plus seam allowance plus ease is less than 45", you can cut this skirt out of a yard or less of fabric. (*See left.*)

Follow the instructions for Straight Skirt, Fitted Waist. (*See page* 18.) *Reminder:* Add ½" to each back piece for the seam allowance. Decide on the length of the skirt, then add ½" for the waistline and 1" for the hem. Cut out three pieces: one front piece on the fold and two back pieces along the selvage.

2. *Overskirt.* There's no need to wash the tulle, as it won't shrink. Since tulle is not a directional fabric, you can cut the second skirt shape upside down. Some tulle is available in 54" widths, so you may need only one length of fabric. (*See left.*)

Instead of drafting a whole new pattern, use the underskirt as a guide (shown as a dotted line at left). Cut the waist edges exactly the same (so the two will fit neatly together), then gradually cut the overskirt slightly larger, especially from the hips down. Add an inch or two on each side by the time you get to the hemline. For an extended hemline, add about 3" to the length of the tulle piece.

PUT IT TOGETHER

1. *Side seams.* Stitch the side seams of the **underskirt**. Finish the seam edges and press them open. Leave the back seam alone.

Sew the side seams of the **overskirt**. These will show through the tulle, so it's best to make tidy ¼" seams. Don't try to press the seams open. They will appear as delicate vertical stripes that add to the style of the skirt.

2. *Back seam.* Prepare for the zipper by marking its length on the back seam of *both* the underskirt and the overskirt; measure from the waist down and place a pin or chalk mark. For the underskirt only, mark up from the bottom of the seam for a slit (ours is 7" long). The wider overskirt does not need a slit.

a. Stitch the **underskirt** from the top of the slit to the bottom of the zipper, backtack, and stop. Leave the zipper part of the seam open. Stitch the **overskirt** from the bottom of the seam (there will be no slit) to the bottom of the zipper, backtack, and stop. Again leave the zipper part of the seam open.

b. To join the skirts at the zipper, turn the tulle overskirt wrong side out and carefully clip the seam at the pin/chalk mark for the bottom of the zipper. Turn the underskirt right side out. Tuck the open seam of the tulle into the open seam of the underskirt.

c. To complete the back seam, turn the underskirt wrong side out (the tulle will be sandwiched inside). Baste a ½" seam to the waistline edge.

3. *Baste waistline seam.* Turn both layers right side out. Baste the two together all around the waistline edge.

4. *Zipper.* Put in the zipper. (*See pages* 39–40.) It's a little trickier with the side seams already sewn, but you can do it. (Now you know why the zipper usually comes first!) Once the zipper is in, open up the basting stitches with a seam ripper and unzip the zipper.

5. *Bias-tape waistband.* Sew on the waistband. (*See pages* 34–35.)

6. *Back slit.* Sew the back slit. (*See page* 85.)

7. *Hems.* Make a ½" double-fold hem on the bottom of the both skirts. (*See page* 28.)

8. *Trim.* Add whatever trim you like. It's easier if you turn the underskirt inside out and pull the skirts apart, so the underskirt doesn't get in the way. To keep the trim going in a straight horizontal line, it's a good idea to measure up from the hem and make a chalk mark all the way around. For a stiff trim like ours, one line of stitching run down the middle of the trim was sufficient.

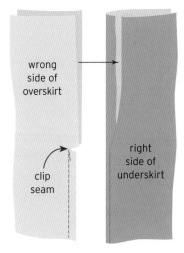

wrong side of overskirt

clip seam

right side of underskirt

STEP 2b

wrong side of underskirt

STEP 2c

*W*HETHER LONG, SHORT, OR LACY, tiers add variety and style to just about any skirt. The simplest version is to add a single ruffle or tier —gathered or not —to the bottom of an A-line top. Once you know how to gather a ruffle, you'll start getting all kinds of ideas!

Multitiered skirts are a bit like a layered cake. The smallest tier is at the top, and each tier below it is larger than the one above. Chances are, you won't make a skirt exactly like any in this chapter. By all means, make up your own design! You can have more tiers or fewer tiers, wide tiers or narrow tiers, more gathers or fewer gathers. Tiers can be different fabrics, all the same fabric, or mostly the same with one odd one thrown in just for fun. As a general rule, it works better to have an odd number of tiers and to make the tiers in varying widths.

Tiers are simple to cut out and easy to sew together. They just take more time, because there are more seams and more fabric to sew. If you like full, free-moving skirts, you'll no doubt find tiers well worth the effort!

East Meets West

Who would think of putting a Wild West retro fabric with an Asian satin brocade? The fabrics are as different as can be, yet the gold colors and brown trim somehow hold it all together. The skirt is simply an A-line, with the bottom part done in a second fabric. A side zipper, a bias-tape waistband, and a strip of brown ribbon complete the project.

Stuff You Need

About 1¼ yards of the primary fabric

About ½ yard of the contrasting fabric

1 spool of matching or contrasting thread

1 matching 7"–9" skirt zipper

1 package of ½" double-fold bias tape

Hook and eye

Enough trim/ribbon for embellishment

What You'll Do

Draft the pattern

Cut out the skirt

Sew contrasting fabric along a curve

Put in the zipper

Straight seams

Bias-tape waistband

Sew the hook and eye

Double-fold hem

Add trim

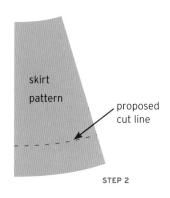

skirt
pattern

proposed
cut line

STEP 2

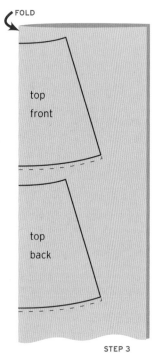

FOLD

top
front

top
back

STEP 3

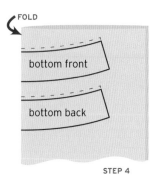

FOLD

bottom front

bottom back

STEP 4

LAY IT OUT, CUT IT UP

1. Wash and press the fabric, then lay it out smooth on a cutting surface. (*See page* 13.) Notice the direction of the nap or pattern design.

2. For this skirt, it would be easier to draft the pattern on paper. Follow the instructions for A-Line Skirt, Fitted Waist. (*See page* 19.) Decide how wide to make the bottom strip of fabric. (The top of our skirt is 19" plus 1" for two seam allowances. The bottom strip is about 3½" plus ½" for the seam allowance and 1" for the hem.) Mark the cutting line along a curve, the same as for the hemline. Cut the pattern along that line.

3. Cut two identical pieces for the top tier of the skirt (front and back). Remember to add ½" at the bottom edge for the seam allowance.

4. Cut two identical pieces for the bottom strip (front and back). Add ⊕" at the top for seam allowance.

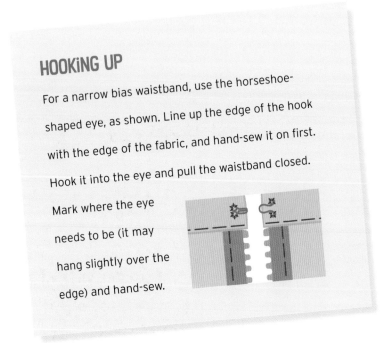

HOOKING UP

For a narrow bias waistband, use the horseshoe-shaped eye, as shown. Line up the edge of the hook with the edge of the fabric, and hand-sew it on first. Hook it into the eye and pull the waistband closed.

Mark where the eye needs to be (it may hang slightly over the edge) and hand-sew.

PUT IT TOGETHER

1. *Attaching the bottom strip.* Staystitch along the top of both the front and the back bottom strips. (*See page* 26.) Sew the front top and front bottom together; then sew the back top and back bottom together. (*See below.*) Press the seams toward the bottom strip and clip the curve if necessary to make it lie flat.

2. *Zipper.* Prepare the left side seam, then put in the zipper. (*See pages* 39–40.)

3. *Side seam.* With right sides together, stitch the right-hand side seam. Try on the skirt and make any necessary adjustments. Finish the seam edges and press the seam open.

4. *Waistband.* Attach the bias-tape waistband. (*See pages* 34–35.) Sew on a hook and eye above the zipper. (*See box on facing page.*)

5. *Hem.* Make a ½" double-fold hem on the bottom of the skirt. (*See page* 28.)

6. *Trim.* Attach the trim. We aligned the bottom of our trim with the seamline between the two fabrics, which helps keep it straight and even.

Fun with Ruffles

skirt top

measure the width

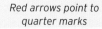

ruffle strip 1

ruffle strip 2

ruffle strip 3

STEP 1

Red arrows point to quarter marks

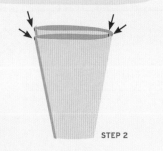

STEP 2

MAKING A RUFFLE is not complicated. Some sewing machines even have a ruffle attachment (check your manual). A ruffle is essentially a long strip of fabric basted on one side, gathered (bunched up) along the basting stitches, then sewn to another piece of fabric. Ruffles can be made of the same fabric as the skirt, a contrasting fabric, tulle, or any number of options.

This skirt is with the same steps as *East Meets West,* except that a gathered bottom strip is added after the zipper is in and the side seams have been sewn. Here's how you make a ruffle.

1. *Measure and cut.* Fabric for a ruffle is usually about two times as long as the edge you sew it to. For example, if the hem edge of the skirt is 33" wide in front, double that to include the back, which equals 66". So, aim for a band of fabric about twice as long: 132". If you're using 45"-wide fabric, divide 132 by 45, which (rounding up) equals three strips of fabric to make the ruffle. (For a more generous ruffle, cut four strips.) Make the ruffle the width you want, adding a ½" seam allowance for the top and 1" for a double-fold hem.

2. *Stitch and mark the strips.* Sew all the strips together end to end, joining them in a continuous loop. Finish the seams and press them open. To help you evenly distribute the gathers, divide the loop into quarters. If you made the loop from four strips of equal length, just use the seams as a guide. Otherwise, fold the loop in half and then in half again. Mark the seam allowance at each of the folds with a fabric marker. Do the same with the skirt, by folding it in half and marking the halfway point between the seams.

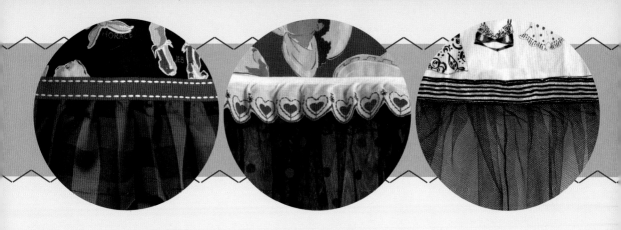

3. Hem it now or later. If you are confident about your measurements and know the length of the skirt will be fine, stitch a double-fold hem on the bottom edge of the ruffle strip before you gather it — unless the bottom strip is tulle, which doesn't need a hem. Or, wait until you've sewn the ruffle to the skirt, so you can adjust the width of the ruffle.

4. Basting stitches. From the right side, along the top edge of the ruffle, stitch two parallel lines of basting stitches (sew the bottom line on the seam-line, and the second line ¼" above it).

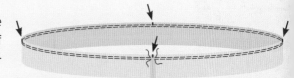

STEP 4

5. Pin and gather the ruffle. Pin the ruffle to the skirt, right sides together, by lining up the four seams and/or marks.

To gather the ruffle, gently pull the fabric along the bobbin threads, then tie the ends of the two bobbin threads together so they won't pull loose. Evenly distribute the gathers between the four marked sections, then pin the ruffle to the skirt.

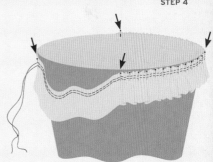

STEP 5

6. Sew on the ruffle. Stitch the ruffle to the skirt, right on top of the bottom basting thread. As you sew, take your time and continuously smooth the ruffle gathers out of the way of the needle (for a smooth seam without bunched-up fabric).

7. Topstitch. Press the seams up, away from the ruffle. Top-stitch with either a straight or a zigzag stitch.

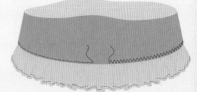

STEP 7

Nature's Child

For tiered skirts, the possibilities are endless. In this variation, a wide bottom tier is hemmed on both sides and sewn on top of the upper tier, creating a narrow ruffle. The same fabric is used for a custom waistband, which tops a side zipper. These fabrics were designed to go together, so the color match, top to bottom, is perfect.

Stuff You Need

2 lengths* of 42"–45" fabric

¼–½ yard of complementary fabric

Interfacing for the waistband

1 spool of thread

1 matching 7"–9" skirt zipper

Hook and eye

What You'll Do

Draft the pattern

Cut out the skirt

Put in the zipper

Straight seams

Custom waistband

Sew the hook and eye

Double-fold hem

Gather and attach the ruffle

Measure the distance from your waist to the desired hemline and add a couple of inches.

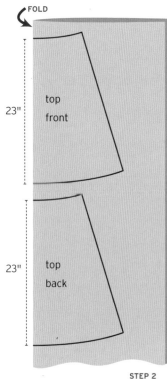

FOLD

23" | top front

23" | top back

STEP 2

LAY IT OUT, CUT IT UP

1. Prepare the fabric according to instructions on the bolt. (*See page* 13.) Notice the direction of the nap or pattern design.

2. *Top of skirt.* Refer to chapter 1 for drafting a pattern to fit your size. Follow the instructions for A-Line Skirt, Fitted Waist. (*See page* 19.) Decide on the length of the top of the skirt, and add 1" for two seam allowances (our top measurement totals 23"). Cut two identical pieces (for the front and the back) from the primary fabric.

3. *Bottom ruffle.* Decide how wide you want the ruffle to be, then add 1½" for the top and 1" for the bottom hem (our bottom measurement totals 9"). *See page* 114 to figure out how long to make your fabric strip; three widths of 45"-wide fabric will probably work fine. Cut the pieces from your complementary fabric.

4. *Waistband.* For a narrow, ¾" waistband, cut a 2½" strip of fabric that is as long as your waist, plus 1" for seam allowances, from your complementary fabric.

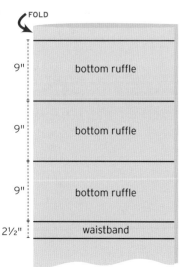

FOLD

9" | bottom ruffle

9" | bottom ruffle

9" | bottom ruffle

2½" | waistband

STEPS 3 & 4

FUZZY RUFFLE

If you like the ruffled edge on this skirt but prefer a more casual style, here's another option. Prepare your ruffled tier as usual, but without turning over the top edge. Sew the ruffle to the top of the skirt layer, as described on the opposite page. What you'll have is a raw edge that will fray over time. This technique works best with a light-weight fabric and looks fabulous on a multi-tiered, gauzy skirt with a fringed hem.

PUT IT TOGETHER

1. *Zipper.* Prepare the left-hand side seam, then put in the zipper. (*See pages* 39–40.)

2. *Side seams.* With right sides together, stitch the right-hand side seam. Try on the skirt and make any necessary adjustments. Finish the seam edges and press the seam open.

3. *Waistband.* Follow the instructions for making your own waistband on page 36. You may want to use interfacing to strengthen the fabric. Sew on a hook and eye above the zipper. (*See sidebar on page* 112.)

4. *Hem.* Make a ½" double-fold hem on what will become the bottom edge of the ruffle. (*See page* 28.)

5. *Making the ruffle.* All along the top edge of the ruffle, fold under and press 1" of fabric. From the wrong side, about ½" from the top edge, stitch two parallel lines of basting stitches. (The basting stitches go through both layers.) Mark four equal sections, as described on page 114. Mark four quarters on the skirt hem as well.

Pin the ruffle onto the top of the skirt (wrong side of the ruffle to the right side of the skirt), matching up the four quarter marks. Gently pull the fabric along the bobbin threads to gather the fabric. Evenly distribute the gathers and pin the ruffle to the skirt every inch or so. To keep the ruffle straight, line up the bottom line of basting stitches on the ruffle with the bottom edge of the skirt top. Pin often. Stitch along the top line of basting stitches, smoothing the gathers out of the way as you go.

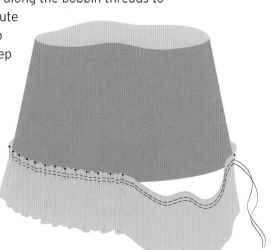

Swing Your Partner

If you like to dance, this is your skirt — full, light, and bouncy! As each tier is fuller than the next, the fabric in each strip adds up. A lightweight option like seersucker is perfect, because it won't weigh you down. The elastic waistline casing is super easy to make and to wear. So, get your dancing shoes ready!

Stuff You Need

42"–45" fabric in the following amounts:

- *Tier 1:* ¼ yard
- *Tier 2:* ⅜ yard
- *Tier 3:* ⅝ yard
- *Tier 4:* ¾ yard
- *Tier 5:* 1 yard

Several spools of matching or contrasting thread

1 yard of ½"–¾" non-roll waist elastic

What You'll Do

Cut the fabric

Straight seams

Elastic waistline casing

Gather and attach the tiers

Double-fold hem

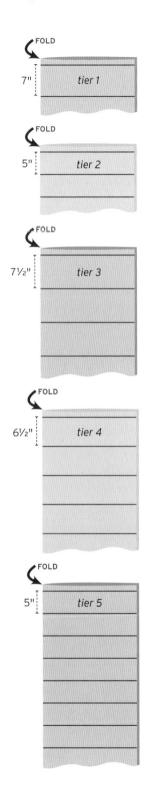

FOLD

7" tier 1

FOLD

5" tier 2

FOLD

7½" tier 3

FOLD

6½" tier 4

FOLD

5" tier 5

LAY IT OUT, CUT IT UP

You will no doubt come up with your own variation on this skirt, but to give you something to go by, here's how to make this one. To figure out how much fabric you need for your own design, sketch it out on paper, like in these diagrams, and do the math. The nice thing about this skirt style is that it's very forgiving. You really don't have to be exact.

1. Prepare the fabrics, as instructed on the bolt. (*See page* 13.) Then lay them out one at a time on a cutting surface.

2. *Tier 1.* The top tier needs to be wide enough to pull on over your hips, plus 2"–4" of ease, plus 1" for seam allowances. If this measurement is less than 45", you can make this tier from one strip of fabric. Decide how long you want this tier to be, then add 1½"–2" at the top for the elastic casing and ½" for the seam allowance at the bottom.

3. *Remaining tiers.* Follow the layout diagrams for cutting instructions. These diagrams show our measurements, but if you want tiers that are longer, buy extra yardage and cut wider strips. Because there are so many tiers in this skirt, it's best not to make every tier twice as long as the one above it, unless you want an exceptionally full skirt.

PUT IT TOGETHER

With so much fabric to sew, make sure you have plenty of thread! It is very frustrating to run out halfway through a long line of basting stitches. You might want to fill two bobbins with thread and check both the bobbin and the spool each time before you start a long row of stitches.

1. *Tier 1.* Stitch the one seam, finish the raw edges, and press the seam open. Make an elastic waistline casing. (*See pages* 32–33.) It might be easier to put the elastic in after you have the rest of the skirt together.

2. *Stitch and mark the strips.* For tiers 2–5, stitch the strips together, and press the seams open. (*See page* 114, *step 2.*) Because some of these tiers are very long, fold each one into eighths (instead of fourths) and mark the folds. For tiers 2–4, mark both top and bottom seam allowances.

3. *Tier 5 only.* Stitch a ¼" double-fold hem along the bottom edge of this tier.

4. *Basting stitches.* For tiers 2–5, stitch two parallel lines of basting stitches along the top of each tier. (*See page* 115, *step 4.*)

5. *Attach the tiers.* You may find it easier to manage the tiers if you start from the bottom up. In other words, match the marks on tier 5 to tier 4; pin, gather, and stitch. (*See page* 115, *steps 5 and 6.*) Then match the marks on tier 4 to tier 3, and so on.

6. *Topstitch.* Press all gathered seams upward, then topstitch the seams. We recommend a zippy zigzag stitch.

7. *Casing.* With a safety pin, thread the elastic through the casing and try on the skirt. Make any necessary adjustments, then finish the casing. (*See page* 33.)

WHATEVER YOU WANT

You can make a perfectly lovely multitiered skirt with as little as three layers. In the version pictured here, the top tier is based on an A-line skirt, with a bias tape waistband and a side zipper. The top tier needs to be at least as long as the zipper, but otherwise the length of the tiers is totally up to you.

Resources

Fabrics, Notions & Tools

The best way to select fabric is hands-on. Check your local phone book under "fabric shops" or "quilting" for local sources of cotton and fashion fabrics, tools, and notions. The following companies are fantastic sources for all your needs and all offer a mail order service. Many of their websites also provide tips, patterns and a lot of great ideas.

Calico Laine
16 Liscard Crescent
Wallasey
Merseyside CH44 1AE
(0151) 638 6498
www.calicolaine.co.uk

Cheapfabrics.co.uk
Thames Court
1 Victoria Street
Windsor
Berkshire SL4 1YB
www.cheapfabrics.co.uk

MacCulloch & Wallis
25-26 Dering Street
London W1S 1AT
(020) 7629 0311
www.macculloch-wallis.co.uk

Online Fabrics
388-394 Foleshill Road
Coventry
West Midlands CV6 5AN
(024) 7668 7776
www.online-fabrics.co.uk

Sunflower Fabrics
5b Dean Street
Bedford
Bedfordshire MK40 3EQ
(01234) 273 819
www.sunflowerfabrics.com

The Sewing Box
50 Newgate Street
Morpeth
Northumberland NE61 1BE
(01670) 511 171
www.sewing-box.co.uk

Sewing Machine Information

If you're looking for a sewing machine manual or need information or parts for your machine, check out the websites below or do a search for the name of your sewing machine manufacturer.

College Sewing Machine Parts Ltd.
Unit 1 Phoenix Park
Phoenix Close
Heywood
Lancashire OL12 2JD
(01706) 623 629
www.college-sewing.co.uk

Sewing Machine Sales
126 Park View
Whitely Bay
Tyne & Wear NE25 3QN
(0845) 430 9824
www.sewing-machine-parts.co.uk

Sewing Parts
14 Copmanswick
Chorelywood
Rickmansworth
Hertfordshire WD3 5JW
(01706) 285 181
www.sewingparts.co.uk

Index

Index *(continued)*